Tweets of a humble pilgrim
A journey of struggling towards God

Father Raphael

Tweets of a humble pilgrim
– A journey of struggling towards God

Copyright©2009–2012 Father Raphael.

Published by Father Raphael Phan
c/o McGallen & Bolden PR Corporation.

All rights reserved. No part of this book may be reproduced in whole or in part without written permission from the publisher, except by reviewers who may quote brief excerpts in connection with a review in a newspaper, magazine, or electronic publication; nor may any part of this book be reproduced, stored in a retrieval system, or transmitted in any form or by any means electronic, mechanical, photocopying, recording, or other, without written permission from the publisher.

ISBN-13: 978-0-9835058-0-8

1. Bible. Interpretation, commentary. 2. Theology. 3. Prayer. 4. Orthodox Christianity. 5. Summary. I. Phan, Raphael. II. Title.

987654321 Printed in the United States of America

With gratitude

This unworthy servant would like to thank: God, He whose Mercy and Love made all things possible even for a grave sinner, the most Holy Theotokos, the many great saints and holy fathers before us who inspired us with their teachings and writings, hierarchs of the Church, fellow pastoral laborers of Christ, and the families. The road is long, and sometimes rocky, but it is such a rewarding journey joyously shared by so many wonderful people. Thank you all, and blessings of our Lord and Christ rest with all of you, always!

Table of Contents

With gratitude 1

Table of Contents 2

Introduction 3

Tweets in a fraction of time 4

More information 132

Introduction

Dear beloved,

Welcome to this pocketbook on some humble and personal reflections using Twitter.

Twitter is an interesting social media platform in that it forces you to write succinctly. You have to distill your thoughts down to the 140 characters it imposes.

The journey of a pilgrim of Christ is lifelong. This is but a fraction of time in the life of a worthless pilgrim of Christ. I hope you will find some bits useful, and perhaps even share some similarities in our mutual journeys as we stumble and struggle towards God. May your spiritual journey be fruitful and blessed, and bring you ever closer to God!

An unworthy servant,

Father Raphael

PS – Do note that this book is purely for a prayerful life towards God. Any external resources provided or presented here, are to help the faithful in their Christian life.

Tweets in a fraction of time

Welcome to the twitter home of our Communion. *– Apr 22, 2009*

The "Old" books described actions, while the "New" described the heart of actions, that transcends mere adherence. *– Apr 23, 2009*

Ever wondered if this vast nature out there means more than what it seems? Therein lies what we are searching for, the Kingdom. *– Apr 23, 2009*

Have you tried a simple experiment, to slow down for just 1 day, to reduce activity, to simply.... listen, observe, and be silent? *– Apr 23, 2009*

IMHO, age is defined as the timeline of wisdom and revelation. Wouldn't it be sad if after a long timeline, one can't find signs of them? *– Apr 23, 2009*

When facing extreme calamity, what do most people do? Rather than lament, why not pray? *– Apr 23, 2009*

An epiphany can be found sometimes at the heart of deep suffering. How we evolve from the suffering determines our eventual journey. *– Apr 23, 2009*

Have you found revelation and epiphany in every breath you take, in every sight and sound of nature, of every footstep around you? *– Apr 23, 2009*

Blessed are the peacemakers... So true, considering the warring and combative stances we face or see every day. – *Apr 26, 2009*

You don't find peace. You merely open your heart wide to invite the peace of the Spirit. – *Apr 30, 2009*

It is important to realize that blessings are not necessarily the obvious. Even adversity can bring out the best (or worst) of men. – *May 01, 2009*

Troubling times we live in, and the duty of the ordained priesthood faces great challenges ahead. – *May 06, 2009*

A Poustinia Day where we find the oasis in the dessert, in a space of enjoying the peace and silence of God. – *May 08, 2009*

Not tears, not death, not sorrow, for the former things are passed away... – *May 14, 2009*

Lest we become Pharisees, let us remember the first signs of being Christian are extending compassion and love. – *May 15, 2009*

True faith is akin to a calm lake, like a mirror. It is hard to find true faith in consuming and fiery fire. – *May 16, 2009*

For whosoever shall do the will of my Father, that is in heaven, he is my brother, and sister, and mother. Mt 12:50 – *May 22, 2009*

No matter how depressed life may seem to some, taking life, sacred as it is, is never the answer. – *May 23, 2009*

Our Lord did not promise an easy path to salvation. Beware of those who promise a wide, open road and cheap grace. – *May 24, 2009*

Angels walk among us, often in guises we may not recognize. Recognize them for the good and our Lord's hidden message. – *May 24, 2009*

There are many who claim to war in the name of God, and distorting the truth within His Word. God is the only and final arbiter. – *May 26, 2009*

Let us, His humble laborers, go forth with the apostolic work of spiritual direction, and not just preaching and hearing confessions. – *May 29, 2009*

Evangelism should not be an application of brute force. After all, God's hands are seen in the most graceful of actions. – *Jun 01, 2009*

Salvation comes to those who seek it. Life as it is, no matter how deep the adversity, should not be an excuse for pity. – *Jun 03, 2009*

Always remember that the Eucharist IS worship, and that Christ is with us. There is nothing more uplifting than a sacramental life. – *Jun 03, 2009*

Remember that noise of any kind, or music, can drown out the subtle voice of God. A quiet contemplative prayer is important. *- Jun 03, 2009*

Imagine a barren desert and a scorching sun. Imagine yourself to be an early Christian on a pilgrimage. What would you do in such adversity? *- Jun 03, 2009*

Our beloved Lord always leaves a door, a window, or a path open to us, even in the worst of adversity. We just have to listen to His voice. *- Jun 04, 2009*

Remember our Lord Jesus Christ going to a mountain to pray all night? Prayer is just so... finding a quiet place to seek our Lord. *- Jun 07, 2009*

The faithful must not use faith as a sledgehammer against others (even against the brethren). Are we showing the love of Christ like He did? *- Jun 13, 2009*

Let us the faithful, build fellow brethren up, and strengthen one another, and be hospitable to all. *- Jun 21, 2009*

"Put not your trust in princes, in the children of men, in whom there is no salvation..." Psalm 146:3 *- Jun 28, 2009*

Our Lord works in mysterious ways. He will use conduits and tools beyond our imagination, to reach His people, to gain disciples of Christ. *– Jul 05, 2009*

Intellectual pride may be a stumbling block to listening to the small voice of God's calling. Sometimes we must shed our pride first. *– Jul 24, 2009*

The Lord delights in those whose hearts are free from envy. *– Jul 30, 2009*

Expecting incessant needs to be filled out of selfish desires is the beginning of the loss of faith. True disciples give, not take. *– Aug 15, 2009*

Sorry for the hiatus. Life can be demanding of our time at times, but even in the busiest of times, remember prayer. *– Sep 01, 2009*

"In the beginning was the Word, and the Word was with God, and the Word was God." John 1:1. Let us reflect on the nature of our Christ. *– Sep 26, 2009*

It is often the hours of darkness that defines our faith in God. Leading a privileged life does not. *– Sep 28, 2009*

Let us transform every element of our life into a sacrament. *– Sep 28, 2009*

If you are looking for an angel with wings, look again. Angels walk among us, often in guises so mundane it is easy to walk pass them. - *Oct 02, 2009*

We need to move from abstract intellectual knowledge (gnosis) to experiential awakening (epignosis) in our search for God. - *Oct 04, 2009*

Our Christ taught us to give hoping for NOTHING in return, which contrasts with what some "teachers" of formulaic giving. - *Oct 05, 2009*

The Biblical parameters for icons can be found in Exodus 25:22 and 26:1, as commanded by God to Moses concerning the tabernacle. Pax Christi - *Oct 08, 2009*

Much as it pains us to confess our sins, remember Matthew 3:6 with St John at the Jordan, and Matthew 16:19 from Christ to Peter. - *Oct 08, 2009*

We must recognize that there is a time for everything, all ordained in our Lord's plan. Read Ecclesiastes 3:1–8. - *Oct 25, 2009*

Often we mortals make life unnecessarily complex because we fear the simple but hard solutions in life. Contemplate on Ecclesiastes. - *Oct 26, 2009*

Let us reflect on 2 Chron 7:14, of the importance of humility in seeking our Lord, and the fruits of prayer it will bring in this manner. - *Oct 30, 2009*

On tradition, let us reflect on 2 Thes 2:15, "So then, brethren, stand firm and hold to the traditions which you were taught by us..." – *Oct 31, 2009*

Care for the poor and needy, "and you will be like a son of the Most High" (read Wisdom of Sirach 4:1–10). – *Nov 01, 2009*

Let us remember St Columcille on his feast day of his life of unceasing prayer and study. – *Nov 12, 2009*

Be gratified that at the time of crucifixion, Dismas who believed in Christ, was saved. In our daily walk, remember not to be like Gestas. – *Nov 17, 2009*

We can expect the journey of faith to be lonely most of the time so that we can get closer to God. – *Nov 17, 2009*

If the world is our cloister let us understand it and not discard it for we are called to service. – *Nov 19, 2009*

"For wisdom is a loving spirit..." Wisdom of Solomon 1:6 – *Nov 19, 2009*

Let us contemplate on as many words that can describe the love of God for us. This unique love described the expression of the Divine. - *Nov 22, 2009*

Let us never stand on our own work and merits, but remember to petition to our God the shed blood of Christ, His expressed grace. - *Nov 23, 2009*

Faith is an evolutionary journey. We brave on, we stumble, and we struggle up again. We simply keep our focus on the way of our Lord always. - *Nov 23, 2009*

"A person is truly pure of heart when he considers all humans as good and no created thing appears impure to him," - St Isaac of Syria. - *Nov 24, 2009*

Let us remember: "And hospitality do not forget; for by this some, being not aware of it, have entertained angels." - Hebrews 13:2 - *Nov 24, 2009*

One of the most heartwarming things an Orthodox priest said to some who embraced Orthodoxy, was "Welcome home". Amen! - *Nov 25, 2009*

It is hard for one at the peak of power and youth, to see the vulnerability of old age. Use our strength and youth wisely for the Lord. - *Nov 25, 2009*

To every journey remember the Desert Fathers, as the harsh and yet purifying terrain would offer. – *Nov 26, 2009*

Heb 13:5 reminds us of the need to have a desire and put to action, to follow the ways of our Lord. – *Nov 28, 2009*

Brethren, remember our goal, that of "theosis", the mystical union of man with God. Embrace the mystery of our faith always. – *Nov 29, 2009*

God yearns to be close to us just as we long to be closer to Him. We can find His presence even when we are simply on a relaxing trip away. – *Dec 08, 2009*

Orthodoxy can be simply described as the adherence to Holy Tradition and Scripture with Apostolic Succession. – *Dec 15, 2009*

"A strong person is the one who chews well, not the one who eats a lot." Elder Paisios of the Holy Mountain. Spirituality is about doing. – *Dec 15, 2009*

Rather than lament over challenges in life, why not view them as road signs? Choose your direction wisely and listen to the voice of God. – *Dec 17, 2009*

Remembering our patron saint for our province, Saint Flannan of Killaloe, Ireland. – *Dec 17, 2009*

"Beside each believer stands an angel as protector and shepherd leading him to life." - St. Basil. *- Dec 21, 2009*

"He cannot have God as a Father who does not have the Church as a mother." - Cyprian of Carthage. *- Dec 24, 2009*

Only by traveling through the insufferable desert (like St Antony), will we be purging our mind and finding pristine clarity to know God. *- Dec 24, 2009*

Let us reflect on Eph 6:10, on how we are called to wear the armor of God against high powers, not of flesh and blood. *- Jan 22, 2010*

Let us consider what God intends us to do, rather than simply adhering to His laws literally. Listen to His heartbeat. *- Jan 23, 2010*

If we view our faith and relationship with God as important, shouldn't we view the Divine Liturgy as instrumental and pivotal to our lives? *- Jan 24, 2010*

Praise the Lord for what we take for granted daily, our breath, our being, our lives, our relationship with the Lord. *- Jan 24, 2010*

Simplistically, the Christian meditation is emptying us and RE-filling with the Holy Spirit, while the Eastern form is about emptying. *- Feb 01, 2010*

Some evangelists are hunters, and not fishers of men. Evangelize kindly, gently, respectfully, wisely, patiently, and biblically. – *Feb 01, 2010*

It is important to us, that our veneration of icons is NOT taken as worship. We only worship our beloved God. Think of national flags. – *Feb 09, 2010*

Remember our Lord the Christ when He proclaimed that the kingdom of heaven is at our doorstep, if only we open our doors (Rev 3:20). – *Feb 17, 2010*

God is like an electrician. He has laid all the wiring and infrastructure beforehand, waiting for His children to just turn on the switch. – *Feb 23, 2010*

Let us remember Jer 6:16, of the ancient paths, and walk in them. Let us return and embrace the ancient paths for the rest we seek. – *Feb 25, 2010*

St Chrysostom observed that God would often send His servants trials to clear their hearts of self-love, but with seasons of consolation. – *Mar 20, 2010*

If Christ were to ask you, "will you be brave enough to follow me? Will you have love enough to follow me?" What would be your answer? – *Apr 16, 2010*

Sometimes we must lose something to gain everything. Let not our ego dictate what we think we have lost, and we may find theosis. – *Apr 26, 2010*

"Theology without action is the theology of demons." Saint Maximus the Confessor. – *May 12, 2010*

There is nothing that pleases the devil more than to bring the servants of God and the Church down. These are visible symbols of the Christ. – *May 18, 2010*

Just as there are false prophets, we must also guard against those with vested interests in pursuing the sacred holy priesthood. – *May 19, 2010*

Our heart is like a clenched fist holding on to gold. Open our fist and relieve it of the burden, and we can find liberation, and God. – May 24, 2010

Some who succumb to the temptations of delusions would imagine incredible religious insight, which alas, does not exist. – *May 28, 2010*

God is often found in the most subtle, most mundane, most often ignored places. Too often people try to find God in the wrong places. – *May 28, 2010*

Let us remember that we are worshipping and growing closer to God, not worshipping men. – *Jun 02, 2010*

Too often, some people imagine their egos and passions as the voice of God, and in turn, lead others to the same sad spiritual destruction. – *Jun 02, 2010*

What the devil does is to erode our faith by showing us how corrupt people of faith seem to be, and make us walk away from God. *– Jun 08, 2010*

Do not be misled by what seems like abundant fruit, for there is good fruit and bad fruit, and God is not after numbers, but humbled hearts. *– Jun 13, 2010*

Stripped of the cloak of power and wealth, all men are but like dirt and debris in the halls of God. Pursue God instead of impostors. *– Jun 17, 2010*

All awards by mortals are transient and meaningless. It is the admission to God's paradise by His love and grace that is most meaningful. *– Jun 19, 2010*

A gift is a present from God, and it is not ours to keep, but to give freely away as a blessing to others. *– Jun 20, 2010*

If things of nature mature in silence, it is no wonder the great saints grew closer to God in silence, and sometimes in desolation. *– Jun 20, 2010*

Every spiritual journey is an important part of a lifetime of pursuit of God. God is everywhere if you care to look and listen hard enough. *– Jun 21, 2010*

Two phrases an Orthodox priest can say that means a great deal to people, "come and see!" and "welcome home!" *– Jun 21, 2010*

An anti-depressant found in every Orthodox Church! Read http://bit.ly/c5NWjo - *Jun 21, 2010*

LXX Ps 90:1 (91) speaks of being in the shelter of our God, where there is all light and warmth, a true lodging of bliss and contentment. - *Jun 21, 2010*

I appreciate and yearn for the narrow gate of Orthodoxy so much more, compared to the seemingly easy and comfortable ways of some. - *Jun 22, 2010*

The most beautiful thing an Anglican said to a person after visiting an Orthodox Church in USA, "there is life there". - *Jun 23, 2010*

Sometimes what we need is to be part of a small, poor, and non-influential church. It is not what we want, but may be just what we need. - *Jun 23, 2010*

A brother said, "are we treating our worship as a cruise ship?" Think like a battleship crew, preparing for war, and everything changes. - *Jun 27, 2010*

Our time is short. Are we to ignore the signs from God, however subtle, simply because our egos chase after mere wealth and power? - *Jun 27, 2010*

Some errantly imagine God to simply be a wish-granting machine. We ought to live for Him, our creator, not the other way around. - *Jun 27, 2010*

Some forgot what "theology" is, a study of God. It's not a study of humans, nor a study of our desires, and certainly not a study of wealth. - *Jun 27, 2010*

The closer you walk towards Orthodoxy (belief), Orthopraxis (action), and Theosis, the more the devil raises stakes against you. - *Jun 27, 2010*

It's sad that some who profess Christ, have no real interest in Him and His Word at all. Salvation doesn't come with a label of "Christian". - *Jun 29, 2010*

"It is not he who begins well who is perfect. It is he who ends well who is approved in God's sight." - St. Basil the Great. - *Jun 30, 2010*

Might and wealth does not make it easy for pursuing the heart of Christ. Christ told us to leave everything behind to follow Him. - *Jul 01, 2010*

In much of life, it seems easy to blame others, and God, for every calamity and pain, when we are responsible ourselves for our errors. - *Jul 05, 2010*

To those who ask why we Orthodox worship liturgically, read Revelation, Isaiah 6, Heb 12:1, 22-24 where our church is a microcosm of Heaven. - *Jul 12, 2010*

To embrace Orthodoxy, you must move away from selectivity (theology & worship) and embrace everything of the Church. There is no "your" way. – *Jul 12, 2010*

Pour out our nous, passions, and will from our heart (like a cup), and let Christ live within our heart, and God's light shine through. – *Jul 13, 2010*

When one's ego rises above that of his perspective of God, it is time to start looking up, and realize that God is way above oneself. – *Jul 21, 2010*

One of the most tragic of spiritual journeys, is to mistake "prelest" as spiritual awakenings. Such "signs and wonders" are but delusions. – *Aug 02, 2010*

Spiritual isolation is not desolation, but rather, a sacred quiet time to shut out distractions for us to listen to the heartbeat of God. – *Aug 22, 2010*

Kind counsel of Bp Kallistos of Xelon, "do not resent. Do not react. Keep inner stillness." – *Aug 24, 2010*

If our egos inflate to the whole of our being and fill it with the incessant noise of ourselves, how can we hear God's gentle voice at all? – *Aug 28, 2010*

Remember our beloved Saint John the Forerunner, as he humbled himself and proclaimed Christ our Lord. Humility is the foundation of truth. – *Aug 29, 2010*

Let's not confuse cowardice with meekness or mere submission. True meekness is humility supported by a fortitude of spirit in inner prayer. - *Aug 30, 2010*

Lord, forgive my many errors, and have mercy on me, a wretched sinner. Lend me Your grace to have just enough strength to walk on everyday. - *Aug 30, 2010*

Saint Alexander Nevsky once said, "God is not found in the strength of numbers." - *Sep 01, 2010*

Don't mistake faith with our passions serving our demons. It is about a difficult and arduous walk towards God for all the breaths we take. - *Sep 12, 2010*

Ignore the loud noises calling for easy journeys. Listen within for the gentle voice of God, calling for a intimate pilgrimage to holiness. - *Sep 12, 2010*

There are no real enemies. Christ said, "Put up again thy sword into its place: For all that take the sword shall perish with the sword." - *Sep 12, 2010*

In the depth of our daily grind, have we forgotten about God? God has been and is always there for us, but where are we when He was there? - *Sep 16, 2010*

Once hatred rises in our hearts, we have left orthodoxy and orthopraxis. The orthodoxy of Christ is that of love for God and one another. - *Sep 24, 2010*

Did we ever wonder, in our daily life, where God was? He was always there in the gentle miracles of the machinery of life and the universe. - *Sep 26, 2010*

In between the cracks of life, God fills them up with His mercy and love. Stand back and see the smoothened walls to see His merciful labor. - *Sep 30, 2010*

The Lord gives, and the Lord takes away. Let us understand how we came, and how we will go. Will today bring us closer to God, or away? - *Oct 03, 2010*

Life has its uneven moments for each person, but death is the only leveler. Are we living every day as God wished for us, or decaying away? - *Oct 06, 2010*

The Lord's merciful miracles are often not thunderous manifestations, but through the simple hands and labors of His faithful people. - *Oct 07, 2010*

God has always been there before us, and is still there with us. It is just us who hasn't found God in all places yet. - *Oct 09, 2010*

While we may be looking for the desert to find God, let us also find God in everywhere He intends us to be – with His children and creation. – *Oct 09, 2010*

Lord, because we are unworthy, lend us Your mercy that we will not collapse under what we ought to do as in Matt 20:26 when serving others. – *Oct 09, 2010*

Nothing moves a person farther away from God and His paradise, than a heart of stone, full of hatred and vindictiveness towards others. – *Oct 09, 2010*

Only the devil will spoil you and allow you to lapse into sin. God's true and abiding love will always have an element of discipline. – *Oct 09, 2010*

Often, the noise of the multitude drowns out the gentle voice of God. – *Oct 10, 2010*

Let us be thankful of the fathers amongst the saints, and our hierarchs, who have lived and affirmed the faith in Christ our Lord. – *Oct 10, 2010*

In times of calamities, let us make an expression of love out of our faith, for those who are God's precious creation as much as we are. – *Oct 10, 2010*

Stand firm in the orthopraxis of showing God's love and truth to those in need, to those in disarray, and to those in the diaspora. – *Oct 10, 2010*

God will only rebuke you like a jeweler laboring gold out of you, while the devil rebuke you like a murderer with poison to snuff life out. - *Oct 11, 2010*

Do not despair, for the holy mystery of reconciliation brings one closer to God, if only we are true and honest with our sins before Him. - *Oct 11, 2010*

Much as St Seraphim of Sarov proposed, our God is where warmth and love is, where the strangely dark and cold evil, does not exist. - *Oct 11, 2010*

Faith cannot be defined by ourselves, or lived the way we want it to be. It should be the Way of God that defines our faith, nothing less. - *Oct 13, 2010*

A contented life like the calm waters, resting in the arms of Christ, is worth much more than pursuing the ever-shifting sands of wealth. - *Oct 13, 2010*

"Mitakuye oyasin", an old Lakota belief that "we are all related", correlates with God's commandment to love our neighbors as ourselves. - *Oct 13, 2010*

When we render service to the community in love and faith, we often end up as the ones who receive the greatest gift of all – love from God. - *Oct 13, 2010*

Encourage one another (Heb 3:13), as fellow pilgrims growing closer to God, and remember that we are all part of the same body of Christ. - *Oct 14, 2010*

Behold the gifts of the Holy Spirit, which are like gentle flowers and the morning dew. Let not the fires of anger kill these gifts. - *Oct 16, 2010*

No matter how small a church is in numbers, she is catholic from the fullness of Divine grace and truth of God, and His holy mysteries. - *Oct 17, 2010*

Let us spring forth love out of faith and truth for others just as our Christ would; and not bitter "faith", nor indulgent "love". - *Oct 17, 2010*

Beautiful prayer of a retired therapist who has early-stage Alzheimer's, "Teach me to be gentle with myself." - *Oct 18, 2010*

Even in the darkest of hours and the worst of suffering, let's pray to our Lord for His mercy and salvation for the sake of others instead. - *Oct 19, 2010*

Lord, when I tread foolishly on the path of darkness, please have mercy on me and reconcile me back to You and lead me back to life again. - *Oct 19, 2010*

Even if the enemy is blatant and obvious, leave the burden with God. Do not let anger and hatred destroy our resting in God's mercy. - *Oct 20, 2010*

Beware beloved, for demons can also create illusory miracles. Be drawn to the life within the Word, and not mere signs and wonders. - *Oct 20, 2010*

When we pray, let us remember there will be moments of bliss and joy, and times of darkness. But let us be vigilant and continue to pray. - *Oct 22, 2010*

God lends His grace to sinners, and by their obedience to Him, can become instruments of His mercy and love to many others. - *Oct 22, 2010*

When confronted with challenges, do we curse and give up, or do we keep a vigilant prayer in our heart and think only of God? - *Oct 23, 2010*

God's earth and its conditions shows us how small we are. Treat His earth with love, reverence, and humility, for we are His stewards. - *Oct 24, 2010*

Sometimes, despite pleas and prayers, we seem not to find God. However, unknown to us, God is supporting our frail bodies right behind us. - *Oct 25, 2010*

Let us make the sign of the Cross frequently, because it reminds us of the carrying of the burden of others as Christ did for all of us. - *Oct 25, 2010*

When God calls us to vocation, it's not a medal or a prize, but faithfully carrying the burden of caring and loving as Christ would for all. - *Oct 26, 2010*

In these times, the demons assail us with their tricks, falsehood, and illusory wonders. Keep walking in prayer and do not get distracted. - *Oct 27, 2010*

As in Matt 7:14, let us not be tempted by easy journeys, for life is found through the narrow gates, forged in our prayers against all odds. - *Oct 27, 2010*

The devil snares us on the journey to God. See our God as a driver and we are on the train. Do not stop or leave the train of salvation. - *Oct 28, 2010*

If you can find even one true spiritual friend sharing the pilgrimage towards God, it will beat hundred others who distract you from prayer. - *Oct 28, 2010*

As Christ taught us, hear the cries of the needy, lend a ready hand in love, and pray for the mercy of God in faith, for we are all His. - *Oct 29, 2010*

Visit the dry, barren desert within us, and plea for the mercy and voice of God, and grant us sight and fortitude in discernment and prayer. - *Oct 29, 2010*

If we should find a saint, it may be someone whom our ego and foolishness have dismissed. Pray for our senses to be humble and faithful. - *Oct 29, 2010*

Light illumines and exposes dust, dirt and trash. Let our inner prayer become our brooms to clean our inner house to be all for God's will. - *Oct 29, 2010*

The litmus test of a Christian is if the person seeks after the fruits of prayer closer to God, or material desires and lures of the devil. - *Oct 30, 2010*

Christ does not want us to baptize non-judiciously, but to disciple people through a slow path of spiritual direction with love and prayer. - *Oct 30, 2010*

All of us are theologians through pious prayer, whether it be the Divine Liturgy, the Jesus prayer, or the sign of the Cross wherever we go. - *Oct 30, 2010*

He who demands incessantly from God receives nothing in faith or consolation. He who asks nothing but mercy from God receives much. - *Oct 30, 2010*

Life is so short, like a ticking timer, to be spent with squabbling with others. Spend time only on God and let Him take care of things. - *Oct 31, 2010*

Lord, give me mercy so that I do not behave like a pharisee, but one after the heart of Christ, in service to others out of faith and love. - *Oct 31, 2010*

Life is surely not a bed of roses, but a Smörgåsbord of many flavors of peace, sorrow, realization, and joy, much like seasons of the year. - *Nov 01, 2010*

The darkest spiritual warfare, is our own inner demons. Lord have mercy on my sins, which are all my doing, and Your grace to set me true. - *Nov 01, 2010*

Dear Lord, the burden of priesthood would have been unbearable if not for the joyful tears You grant us on the altar. With grateful tears... - *Nov 02, 2010*

Lest the ego deludes us thinking we are fools for Christ, discern whether deep down, God is our rudder and master, or just our own will. - *Nov 02, 2010*

Before we pick up a stone to aim at others, consider that we can be a stone that hurts, or a rock of faith for God and strength to others. - *Nov 02, 2010*

Do not lament in suffering, no matter how long, for God wants to smoothen our rough edges into smooth pebbles as the ground to serve others. - *Nov 02, 2010*

Always remember the Church that gave us the Holy Scripture, and its Sacred Tradition. Lean on it, embrace it, grow in it, live it, love it. – Nov 04, 2010

Nothing professes our faith more visibly, and more evangelically, than the sign of the Cross, our Icons, daily rule, and the Divine Liturgy. – *Nov 04, 2010*

I thank God for His mercy, for Christ chose ordinary men, and they walked in the heart of Christ. May our Lord grant us mercy to theosis. – *Nov 06, 2010*

When we are parched in the desert, remember that God intends that we are strengthened by faith and prayer, not just on consolations. – *Nov 06, 2010*

God's grace is not intended to satiate our material desires and passions, but to lean us closer to Him so that we may receive salvation. – *Nov 06, 2010*

My Lord and God, grant me Your mercy, that I will only look at my own infinite sins, and be granted strength, and focus on prayer to You. – *Nov 06, 2010*

Let us keep our Lord's words, in Matt 19:23–24, to our hearts, that we will always keep the Way and Love of Christ foremost, and not wealth. – *Nov 07, 2010*

Blood and water, a little like blood on our worn feet, and tears on our eyes, as we remember Christ who gave us reconciliation back to God. - *Nov 07, 2010*

Let hearts never out of pride deny the seekers of the Truth; and also hearts never out of pride deny the Truth and the pilgrimage to God. - *Nov 07, 2010*

Much of our intended spiritual pilgrimage must be lonely journeys like the Desert Fathers. Lord, grant us mercy and theosis in our prayers. - *Nov 08, 2010*

Dew is unlike the ocean, and yet the same substance. If we are in the desert, even a drop of dew is enough, just as our Lord's mercy is. - *Nov 08, 2010*

Often, God's consolations shine from simplicity, gentility, and honesty. God does not tempt with grandeur. God will never lead you to sin. - *Nov 08, 2010*

Let us not be tempted to look for grand illusions in the desert, but rather, praying for an inner strength to brave on, a mercy by God. - *Nov 08, 2010*

Do not bear hatred for those who do evil against others, but pray to our Lord and God for their repentance, redemption, and reconciliation. - *Nov 08, 2010*

If one's ego rises to the surface amidst what seems like a stoic and almost harsh faith, it is not foolishness-for-Christ, but a poor copy. - *Nov 09, 2010*

Like the Russian pilgrim, how much baggage do we lug around? The less we carry, the less we desire, the more time we have to pray to God. - *Nov 09, 2010*

I am grateful for the consolations of God along a journey that a weakling like me find difficult. God, grant me strength, in Your mercy. - *Nov 10, 2010*

God hears our prayers from a true heart. He is unbiased to volume, language, race or place. Consider the Jesus Prayer that anyone can pray. - *Nov 11, 2010*

The devil is especially ferocious when we pray to God. Even saints struggle against such obstacles. Do not stop praying even facing death. - *Nov 11, 2010*

The devil incites pride as his weapon against the rich, and the poor. Our weapons? The Church, the Word, Sacraments, and our humble prayer. - *Nov 11, 2010*

Do not despise the so-called "least" among us, for they may be saints or even Christ Himself. Welcome and tend to them with faith in love. - *Nov 12, 2010*

If our Lord's mercy has granted you strong shoulders, they are meant to carry the burden of many others. Rely on prayer and faith forward. - *Nov 12, 2010*

An Orthodox abbot once said, that if we'd only focus on our own sins and not the sins of others, we would progress spiritually towards God. - *Nov 13, 2010*

The brightest light casts the harshest shadows. Likewise, God's light can bring to light the deepest of sins to allow us to repent and pray. - *Nov 14, 2010*

Lord, please strip my pride away, for it is the disruptor of my journey to You. Give me sight to always see this beast in whatever guise. - *Nov 15, 2010*

We must remember that all humans err, but the Love and Ways of our Lord and Christ never change. Consider all things in faith and love. - *Nov 17, 2010*

If the Lord truly has called you, it is He whom you labor for, it is His mercy who endures, it is His strength who empowers you to go on. - *Nov 18, 2010*

If you feel alone as a pilgrim, do not despair, and do not be afraid, for God has always been with you, even if it is not apparent. - *Nov 19, 2010*

Beloved, the Church should not sway to our passions, but serve as a challenging and curative place for us to feel the heartbeat of God. - *Nov 22, 2010*

In our perceived sorrows let us wipe our tears because we are still conscious and able to pray unto God, for His mercy is a mystery. - *Nov 22, 2010*

Christ is a step away, a breath ago, because He is ever present, if we slow down, be still, and let our humble prayers reach out to Him. - *Nov 22, 2010*

Who are we, sinners all, to judge others? God is the only and final arbiter. In all things, love God, and love others, as Christ commanded. - *Nov 22, 2010*

Lest we fall to the evil one like Pharisees, judge not others, love all, and most of all, pray like penitents unto God with love and faith. - *Nov 23, 2010*

The fruits of faith in God is seen from our character. Do you see anger and hatred? That is the work of the evil one. Or do you see love? - *Nov 25, 2010*

Hatred fosters hatred, and taints the heart which belongs to God. Love fosters forgiveness, peace, joy, and love, which God desires of us. - *Nov 25, 2010*

When we quote the Bible or the saints, we are judged by our hearts, and not mere words. Even the devil twists Holy Scripture to his deeds. – *Nov 25, 2010*

It is wonderful when God sends His gentle saints, to remind us of our failings, but in a gentle way that we sit up and listen. – *Nov 27, 2010*

In all prayer, remember that the devil's prelest can insidiously sneak in, if you are only seeking signs and wonders, and not God Himself. – *Nov 29, 2010*

Consider this when weighing all things against Matt 22:36–40, do we love God above all things, and do we love others as ourselves? – *Nov 29, 2010*

Life as God ordained it, is not as complicated as we pretentiously try to mould it into. Learn from the pious saints who led simple lives. – *Nov 29, 2010*

Even as we face fatigue, let us remember St Paul's admonition, to brave on, to finish the race, for salvation is as long a journey as life. – *Dec 01, 2010*

Those who arm themselves with swords will face swords against them, while those who give food and clothing, will face tears of joy. – *Dec 01, 2010*

Our beloved Christ did not say, "love yourself", nor did He say "punish others". He wanted us to love God, and others – "just" two laws. – *Dec 02, 2010*

Christ opened His arms in love to everyone. He was not a gatekeeper. He told us to love God and love all, not love some and hate others. - *Dec 04, 2010*

All of us are merely partakers of the Mysteries of God's salvation. We cannot confine or define who, where, what, when and how He saves. - *Dec 05, 2010*

We are called to vocation by God's grace, as physicians, counselors, teachers, servants, and brothers to all - not as executioners or judges. - *Dec 06, 2010*

Never forsake love and faith, even if the enemy provokes you to hatred and anger. For only love and faith in God make you Christian. - *Dec 08, 2010*

Everything we do thinking about God at the same time, becomes a prayer unto Him. Everything else without thinking of Him is empty. - *Dec 09, 2010*

Never despair in any condition, look to Him. Always pray with joy, for to be able to pray is itself a merciful blessing and grace of God. - *Dec 09, 2010*

God gave us free will. Will we find His Kingdom in our hearts with bliss and tears of joy? Or do we create a hell ourselves to dive into? - *Dec 09, 2010*

God did not create us with eyes on the back of our heads to lament. We are to look ahead, lean on Him, and seek Him always in prayer. *- Dec 09, 2010*

Don't reduce God to merely an equal opposite to the devil. The devil's just a created being. God is infinite, above all and creator of all. *- Dec 09, 2010*

If you have a wound, let it heal, pick yourself up, and trusting in the mercy of God. Never aggravate or wail about a wound again and again. *- Dec 10, 2010*

It's sad if we're given the gift of Truth of God, but shuns it out of pride, or loses it out of a lack of love for God and all His creation. *- Dec 12, 2010*

Fortify yourself by a penitent prayer when in despair and never lose hope, for despair is the most common trick of the evil one. *- Dec 16, 2010*

Pray with tears, ask God for discernment in all things, and leave all your baggage and burden with Him. Abide in Him, and by His time. *- Dec 17, 2010*

God gave us a cold winter not to feast and hide in our warm homes, but to seek out our brethren freezing and hungry, and care for them. *- Dec 18, 2010*

In the cold winters, we are called to reflect and pray for a warm heart, ready for others, and embracing the journey ahead in the new year. - *Dec 18, 2010*

Beloved, the mustard seed, is foremost referring to our interior life towards God, and not just aggressively trying to change others. - *Dec 18, 2010*

Humans will often trip over themselves. Do we trip together, or pray unto the Lord for mercy, and help them up with love and faith instead? - *Dec 21, 2010*

Beloved, always remember the heart of Christ, and St John the Beloved. Are we leaning on His heart as the center of all things in our life? - *Dec 21, 2010*

Christ can be found at the most mundane, simple, humble places and people. Do not be dazzled by the evil one's acts. Discern and pray. - *Dec 21, 2010*

Be grateful, for all things are ordained by God. His mercy is a mystery, and we need to abide by faith, not fear, and constant prayer. - *Dec 21, 2010*

Even things seemingly from God must be measured against Scripture, discerned through humble prayer, and with a spiritual director. - *Dec 29, 2010*

If even for the slightest moment you sense an unnatural passion of pride, then whatever you are doing is no longer in the path of God. – *Dec 29, 2010*

When things seem unnecessarily challenging, discern and pray humbly, for it may be God's sign for us to move in another way without pride. – *Jan 01, 2011*

God's plans for everyone are unique. If you discern, pray with utmost humility, you will hear His voice distinctly. Do not be misled away. – *Jan 01, 2011*

Observe the elements and places around you. If you look and listen gently and humbly enough, you will find God in all places, at all times. – *Jan 02, 2011*

We don't define who, where, when, and how God is. He defines all things, all places, all beings, all of time. He transcends all – a Mystery. – *Jan 02, 2011*

Beloved, the evil one has many tricks; such as incite hatred in us. Hatred detaches us from God completely as it is void of the Holy Spirit. – *Jan 02, 2011*

In life, we can do it our way, or God's way. If we do it God's way, all we can do is trust and love Him, love others, be humble, and pray. – *Jan 03, 2011*

If we love God, we will love others as ourselves. If we cannot love others, walk away without a fight, and pray with tears for His mercy. *- Jan 03, 2011*

Every being is a creation of God. Nothing will change that reality. We can choose to ignore that only because of our pride and blindness. *- Jan 03, 2011*

Beloved, don't confuse prideful pity as kindness. Kindness is abundant in love and humility, seeing everyone as a priceless creation of God. *- Jan 03, 2011*

In the mental and spiritual dimensions of our hearts, are we giving Christ the entire space across time, for the immense joy and peace? *- Jan 03, 2011*

Don't be blinded by God's immense light because we raised our heads high. Rather, lower ourselves in humility to enjoy His light and warmth. *- Jan 03, 2011*

If we only see the sins of others, it's merely a mirror exposing our own decay. Let us be blind to the ills of others, but repent our own. *- Jan 04, 2011*

Why do we find joy when the Holy Spirit is near? It is because God is infinite joy and love. If you experience otherwise, it is not of God. *- Jan 04, 2011*

Beloved, let us remember the lessons of Job, is not about passing a test to gain more, but that of spiritual purity, humility, and faith. *- Jan 05, 2011*

The heart of Christ is unlike our frail hearts that sometimes have momentous pity for others. His heart is one of undying love for all. *- Jan 05, 2011*

The "rewards" of the world are fruits of the evil one. They embolden, weaken, and lure the person to be arrogant, critical of his brethren. *- Jan 05, 2011*

Christ is God, and so He does not carry emotive variance and irrational outbursts. Lean on His heart to find that it is simply love and joy. *- Jan 05, 2011*

Beloved, our path is about God, with God. It's not a journey for worldly recognition. The reward is simply walking besides God on the way. *- Jan 05, 2011*

Beloved, my humble "daily challenge" is: Have I slowed down for God today? Have I found God today? Have I seen His gentle signs today? *- Jan 05, 2011*

The evil one laughs with contempt, at how we fall into the lure of anger and hatred, even in pain. Our solace? Prayer with tears to God. *- Jan 05, 2011*

Too often, we create God in our own myopic minds, imagining Him to be much less. God created all, knows all things, and reaches out to all. *- Jan 05, 2011*

Since only one can occupy the seat in your heart, would you rather have the Holy Spirit there, or the evil one? It is one's own choice. *- Jan 06, 2011*

A heart is like a house. With God as centerpiece, you will have a big heart, very few furniture, and a front porch welcoming the sun's rays. *- Jan 06, 2011*

How to be FREE? Faith in God; Rest in the Holy Spirit; Emulate the walk of Christ; Empathy for every single person, friendly or otherwise. *- Jan 06, 2011*

When we are hurried and overly occupied with all tasks (even religious) out of pride, we become insensitive to God's subtle calls to us. *- Jan 07, 2011*

Abide in the law to love all others as ourselves because we love God. We are all sacred creations of God, worthy of love, and loved by God. *- Jan 07, 2011*

Beloved, take your time to examine the Footprints of God in nature – a flower, a shrub, a tree, sunlight, rain, earth, water, or people. *- Jan 09, 2011*

Our relationship with God cannot be occasional, nor is it slavery. If we humbly sit with Him, it is truly liberating and abundantly joyous. *- Jan 09, 2011*

A relationship with God is like good Japanese green tea, while a relationship with the evil one is like artificially sweetened beverages. *– Jan 09, 2011*

Christ would lay His life for all, and He loves all. Do we break down all barriers to love like He would, or wall ourselves away from all? *– Jan 09, 2011*

True mercy for others is not prideful pity, but sacrificial love that gladly gives all, out of faith and love for God and His ways. *– Jan 10, 2011*

Those who have crossed the desert of cold nights and scorching heat, appreciate the infinite mercy and love of God, and pray with tears. *– Jan 10, 2011*

Even a grain of sand tells much: Faith like a rock (hard), part of the community (the desert), from trials to theosis (polishing to shine). *– Jan 11, 2011*

A drop of water tells much: Abiding in God's will (pliable), indivisible of Christ's Body (whole ecosystem), can be transfigured (to vapor). *– Jan 11, 2011*

We, the ordained laborers, are held to at least 2 of His laws, embracing His blinding love with joy, and to extend our pastoral love to all. *– Jan 11, 2011*

The closet is a wondrous place, for it blinds us to the temptations of the world, and turns our attention only to God in silence and prayer. *– Jan 12, 2011*

The test is when we are in dire need, who will come to our aid expecting nothing? Only those of the heart of Christ stay, out of agape. *– Jan 13, 2011*

Beloved, do not be afraid in a lonely journey finding God, for I truthfully tell you, He has been with us all along even as we are blind. *– Jan 13, 2011*

Beloved, pray to God for us be blind to faults of others, deaf to malice, mute to evil speech, and dead to the temptations of the evil one. *– Jan 14, 2011*

God is the trainmaster and we are on His train. Talk to Him, enjoy the journey where He leads us home. Don't be misled to get off the train. *– Jan 14, 2011*

If you seek God truly, you will find Him everywhere. If you seek Him not, even if He is right in front of you, you will not realize it. *– Jan 14, 2011*

God gave His priests the burden of love, so that they can bring His laws, His Truth, His love, and most of all, His salvation, to all. *– Jan 15, 2011*

Nothing extreme, harsh, cold, and distant is of the heart of Christ our Lord. Beloved, discern, humbly pray, and you will see the Truth. *– Jan 15, 2011*

It is a painful and tiring journey running away from God's constant yearning and love for us. It is fruitful, if we just stop and go to Him. *– Jan 15, 2011*

Do not deride the mystery of God's specific grace and mercy to others. Edify and pray for them, thanking God for His mercy. *– Jan 15, 2011*

Often, we imagine bliss to be found afar, in some idyllic or sacred places. But if we have Christ in our hearts, bliss is wherever we are. *– Jan 17, 2011*

God's Truth and Light shines ever so painfully, but His mercy prevails and it is easy to see the truth, and head towards His tender call. *– Jan 17, 2011*

Beloved, the evil one can work so insidiously on our pride that we may even believe we do everything for the glory of God. Discern and pray. *– Jan 17, 2011*

Measure every deed not against mere words of men, but against their hearts laid bare before God. Find light, faith, and tender love? *– Jan 17, 2011*

The wind tells much: Praying silently (stillness), laboring with love for the needs of others (movement), strength through God (magnitude). *– Jan 17, 2011*

The soil tells much: Carrying the Cross (foundation), helping others grow their faith (nutrients), humbly accepting Lord's mercy (earthen). *– Jan 17, 2011*

Our feet can be a reflection of our faith in God. Do we have light steps, walking a joyous dance of life? Or do we drag our feet around? - *Jan 18, 2011*

It is an uphill, fruitless struggle when we go against God's best intentions out of love. Instead, let us drop our wills and simply follow. - *Jan 19, 2011*

When our desires, no matter how rational or even seemingly religious, rise ahead of us - stop, pray, and await God's voice to rule again. - *Jan 19, 2011*

Beloved, is something troubling you? Our God has already known the outcome of your journey. Pray unto Him, and leave your burden with Him. - *Jan 20, 2011*

God's love, like the light of a blazing sun, is universal and without bias. He loves all of His creation, if only they would walk to Him. - *Jan 20, 2011*

The evil one wields the weapon of despair. Beloved, remember that despair has no power over the penetrating, warm and curative love of God. - *Jan 20, 2011*

Beloved, do not neglect or despise the grains of sand of the broken Body of Christ, for each is a precious pearl loved by God tenderly. - *Jan 21, 2011*

Beloved, walk every morning as a daily pilgrimage – to find the subtle, almost indiscernible footprints of God everywhere, and walk in them. *– Jan 21, 2011*

Beloved, we love and appreciate the beauty of flowers. But consider also, that even a blade of weed, is a creation of God, for His purpose. *– Jan 21, 2011*

If we feel as if God does not love us, or love us less, it is merely because we are walking away from Him. His love for us never changes. *– Jan 22, 2011*

Ever fell on slippery rocks covered with moss? A true rock of faith is free from the moss of pride, so that it benefits others with love. *– Jan 22, 2011*

Every journey begins not with a dream or fortitude, but one of silent prayer, sitting quietly with God, and humbly listening to His voice. *– Jan 22, 2011*

When we put aside our own pride and biases, and begin to see everyone as an icon of Christ, we too, will be transfigured towards Theosis. *– Jan 22, 2011*

Beloved, let us tend to and nurture the humble gardens in our yards, remove the weeds, and do rest a little sometimes and look skywards. *– Jan 22, 2011*

Beloved, do not be afraid, when Christ calls you to follow Him, for He walks with you on a journey that strengthens and moulds you for God. *- Jan 22, 2011*

Beloved, try this daily. Rise early, open the windows, breathe deeply, and watch the sun rise in the East. A marvel of God's mercy, daily. *- Jan 22, 2011*

Beloved, take a moment, and sit quietly to watch the evening sun as it sets. As the darkness falls, reflect on the mercies of God, today. *- Jan 23, 2011*

Beloved, when faced with a dilemma, the path abiding by God's will is usually not the easy one. Pray, listen to Him, and do not be afraid. *- Jan 23, 2011*

A true soldier of Christ, even if carrying a sword on his back, carries it like the burden of love and faith of the Cross, and not to harm. *- Jan 23, 2011*

Beloved, God does not reject us because of the simplicity of our prayers due to the lack of means. He is after our hearts, not our wallets. *- Jan 23, 2011*

What do you see in the word "face"? I see "faith", "action", "courage" & "empathy". Anything can be God's subtle voice, when we are humble. *- Jan 23, 2011*

All too often, when Christ welcomes us with open arms of salvific love, we reject Him because we want something more glamorous and worldly. – *Jan 23, 2011*

Beloved, do we recognize the face of Christ? All too often, we walked by and ignored Him, because we expected someone of our own liking. – *Jan 23, 2011*

Our spiritual life with God is like a lake. It can be frozen and dead. It can be torrential and harmful. Or, it can be calm and alive. – *Jan 23, 2011*

Beloved, do not despair when nights are long and cold, for the Lord our God leaves gifts of mercy to allow us to survive through such times. – *Jan 25, 2011*

Beloved, dark nights of the soul are but precursors to the morning sun, the early dew, the cool breeze, the calm sounds of running waters. – *Jan 25, 2011*

Allow the Word of God to still you, and awaken you. Let not your own will and voice drown your time with God because of impatient arrogance. – *Jan 25, 2011*

True discernment is God's gift that steels our resolve to walk a challenging path, despite temptations and empty promises of the evil one. – *Jan 25, 2011*

In all things beloved, pray not for rewards, but God's mercy, discernment, discipline, faith, and inner prayer. Those are true gifts of God. *- Jan 25, 2011*

When we behold Christ and His heart deep in our own hearts, all the Laws of God will naturally follow, and we abide in Him as He in us. *- Jan 25, 2011*

Every new day is a gift of mercy from God to allow us to grow yet closer to Him. Do we remember Him today, whether in leisure, or labor? *- Jan 25, 2011*

There is a reason why our baggage is heavy – because we are hanging on to them. And when our burden is light? Carry some of others' burden. *- Jan 25, 2011*

True faith and holy purpose elude one whose heart reeks of harshness and pride, sadly to be devoured easily by the delusions of the devil. *- Jan 26, 2011*

Warmly give tender love and gentle guidance to our spiritual children, and let God's mercy guide them in His Ways, for we are sinners too. *- Jan 26, 2011*

The fall due to anger and hatred is worse than apathy, for rage erases reason, faith and love. Do not be tempted so. Withdraw and pray. *- Jan 26, 2011*

Beloved, don't take each day in vain as life is transient. Treasure it, live it fully for God's glory, and grow in faith, and love others. *- Jan 27, 2011*

Beloved, truly everyone is an icon of Christ. Do not disregard anyone out of pride. God's grace is far reaching, far more than we imagine. *- Jan 27, 2011*

Spiritual myopia is an impediment to Theosis, and removes us from God's children, and worse, from God Himself. God reaches out to everyone. *- Jan 27, 2011*

There are many things admonished unto us by Saint Paul the Apostle, one of which is to focus on the important, not the shadows of things. *- Jan 27, 2011*

God does not force us to submission. He walks, woos, and yearns for us to reach to Him. And He does give His mercy freely and joyously. *- Jan 27, 2011*

We try to strip harshness out of our speech and with God's mercy, out of our hearts, as pastors. For Christ our Lord showed the Way. *- Jan 27, 2011*

My Lord and God, my legs are tired. I am grateful for the merciful rest You give me, and the Fatherly grip to pull me up to walk again. *- Jan 27, 2011*

To every uphill climb that pains us, God mercifully gives us an occasional consolation downhill after the summit. The journey goes on. - *Jan 27, 2011*

Dear God, grant me these gifts: Faith, strength, discernment, compassion, tenderness, blindness to bias, and love. In Christ I ask, amen. - *Jan 27, 2011*

Charity begins in the heart. It starts with tears, silent prayer, and then action. Let God lead us, and we meekly and selflessly follow. - *Jan 27, 2011*

When God truly sits in our hearts and we lean on Him, you find a radiating warmth and tenderness that yearns to warm and comfort others. - *Jan 27, 2011*

If we can spread His Word, do so in love. If not, encourage. If not, good humor. If not, a listening ear. If not, then keep silent. - *Jan 27, 2011*

As priests, we are to be brothers to the inflamed, servants to the poor, healers to the sick, and teachers of His love to all our children. - *Jan 27, 2011*

When God shows His face to us through gentle signs and people, you can't help but marvel and bow at such purity, kindness, warmth, and love. - *Jan 28, 2011*

Life is not cast in stone. Allow God to reveal subtle signs, walk slowly, stop at times, pray humbly, ask for His mercy, and follow Him. *– Jan 28, 2011*

God reminded me today, that the saints He sent to rescue me in my trials of fire many years ago, deserve my love, always. I do, always will. *– Jan 28, 2011*

God is our final arbiter to our spiritual journey towards Him, and He alone knew and carefully tends to our journey, in ways beyond us. *– Jan 28, 2011*

Tears are a gift from God when we weep with joy at the mercy of God. But pull away from tears of sadness that spring from a wrong place. *– Jan 29, 2011*

Beloved, do not be afraid of finding a calm silence in your heart. God is there in that silence. It is noise that clouds and deludes us. *– Jan 29, 2011*

Beloved, before we ask God yet another demand, perhaps we could stop, discern and discover all that we can find contentment today instead. *– Jan 29, 2011*

When we imagine Christ being hidden from us, it is because we have closed the door to His open and warm heart. He is only a doorknob away. *– Jan 29, 2011*

Beloved, God has distinct plans for every single person. To question Him why is akin to not having faith in His providence, mercy and love. – *Jan 29, 2011*

Don't let ambition become a stumbling block to our journey towards God. God doesn't care for mortal desires, but how our hearts lean on Him. – *Jan 29, 2011*

Do not let labels become our blindness. Rather, let our hearts become the light and healing of Christ to permeate to all that He loves. – *Jan 29, 2011*

Gray skies and stormy weather are but transient. What follows will always be bright sunny days of God's healing light and warm love for us. – *Jan 29, 2011*

In my cry to the Lord He said: you are My laborer, feed the hungry, tend to the needy, pray often, love all in your path, that is all. – *Jan 29, 2011*

Discern in silent prayer, God's opening of specific doors and specific people He placed in our lives. Each door or person is a Divine will. – *Jan 29, 2011*

Christ did not preach a combatant faith. Rather, He is the epitome of peace, compassion, forgiveness, faith, selfless sacrifice, and love. – *Jan 29, 2011*

The enigma of Christ's face is that it is at once filled with compassion, a tender smile, and a penetrating gaze that melts distractions. – Jan 29, 2011

What do you find when you can see the heart of Christ? Blinding light you adjust to, intense warmth that envelops you, and a loving calm. – Jan 29, 2011

Beloved, do not neglect the power of what seems like the simplest prayer, "Lord Jesus Christ, Son of God, have mercy on me, a sinner". – Jan 30, 2011

Beloved, it is a sin to imagine the Holy Spirit is limited in power, and limited by human boundaries, in the working of miracles and faith. – Jan 30, 2011

My Lord and God has brought me back to the tranquil state I was in, because I now know what He intends me to do next. I will follow Him. – Jan 30, 2011

Beloved, look hard and deep at the expressions, for they speak of the inner person. Christ showed us the Way, of faith, kindness, and love. – Jan 30, 2011

All who are called to vocation serve God's Divine purpose, and not of their own, but a selfless love built on a tender heart of faith. – Jan 30, 2011

Think of a person as a pond. Is it agitated and furious? Or is it calm and tranquil, warm, full of clarity and abundant life living within? - *Jan 30, 2011*

Christ said, look for Him where there are signs of His sacrifice, peace, warmth and love. He said, follow Him, and not the harsh shadows. - *Jan 30, 2011*

God has sent His saints and angels among us, and those are easy to find, if you allow them to exhibit their tender gestures with warm hands. - *Jan 30, 2011*

Much can be learned from the dance of life, where you face the light of truth and love, and shy away from the harsh shadows that wound. - *Jan 30, 2011*

Thanks be to my God, He who rescued me from much disturbances, and to spur me on with renewed strength, to continue His tasks. I am His. - *Jan 30, 2011*

To every journey and twist on the road, there is God's message, and lessons to be learned well, whether painful or peaceful. And move on. - *Jan 30, 2011*

Beloved, do not view challenges as bitter pills. Rather, view such as Divine callings to strengthen you, for a better journey ahead to God. - *Jan 30, 2011*

Do not curse or disavow every difficult step in our journeys, for each step can be a foundation, as long as our heart is towards God always. – *Jan 30, 2011*

God's mercy is immense, as His saints are true and enveloping in their expression of the heart of Christ – that of kindness and love. – *Jan 30, 2011*

If others are arrogant, do not confront them with anger or pride. Walk away with humility and let the prayer of the heart be your comfort. – *Jan 30, 2011*

Everyone is a child of God, even if they don't recognize it yet. God yearns for everyone to return to His arms in love. Let's pray for this. – *Jan 30, 2011*

Even saints have flaws as Divine providence to keep them as saints. We are only to focus on our own sins and flaws, and not to judge anyone. – *Feb 02, 2011*

True purity of the heart is often found in people who are among us, ignored by us. They are saints who quietly do God's work in our midst. – *Feb 02, 2011*

Trust in our God, who is the master of all, even in the midst of pains, ills, and struggles. His will is a mystery, but for us to follow. – *Feb 02, 2011*

When the faithful fight among themselves over nuances, the Spirit is lost in them, and Christ grieves. Do we dwell on nuances, or on God? - *Feb 02, 2011*

Do not carry the burdens of history or hate it, for God's will is found there to refine and strengthen us. Walk always in love and light. - *Feb 02, 2011*

God is universal and without bias, and He gives His grace and love to all, whatever form or origin we are. Respect and abide in His will. - *Feb 02, 2011*

It is not ours to judge anyone. But for spiritual growth, always first seek the heart of Christ, discern, pray, and find the illumined path. - *Feb 02, 2011*

The rock of faith is not stubborn or biased, but one of fortitude in substance to the Lord, and smooth edges of love and kindness to all. - *Feb 02, 2011*

Even the dimmest stars are bright. It is us who divorce ourselves far away not to recognize them. God is the same. Are we near Him? Or far? - *Feb 02, 2011*

When the Holy Spirit is with you in your prayerful pilgrimage towards God, the experience is more profound than simply studying theology. - *Feb 03, 2011*

The time is coming when men will go mad and when they see someone who is not mad they will attack him for being different. Anthony of Egypt. – *Feb 03, 2011*

Our hearts can be filled with any 4-letter word: bias, cold, defy, dull, feud, hate, hell, pain, vain. Let it be filled with "love" instead. – *Feb 04, 2011*

The mark of a saint is love – that is warm, consuming, illuminating. It has none of the fuzziness, bias, vanity, or coldness of the world. – *Feb 04, 2011*

Beloved, do not lose faith in trying circumstances, for our God shines His light in the darkest corners. Be still, and He is there with you. – *Feb 06, 2011*

God sees us through our hearts, not just exhibited actions. Bring only actions of faith and love for others, and leave all else to God. – *Feb 06, 2011*

The intent of the evil one is to incite hatred in us, for hatred reduces us to mere minions of him, and removes us from the grace of God. – *Feb 06, 2011*

Beloved, still our hearts, so that they may strip their passions behind, and resonate only in the remembrance of, and the prayer unto God. – *Feb 06, 2011*

For all worldly desires, even those outwardly ecclesial, end in nothing. The only thing that matters is our embrace with Christ for life. - *Feb 06, 2011*

Beloved, do not be deluded by the evil to focus on the outer person, in whatever dressing, when the innermost heart is dull and cold to God. - *Feb 06, 2011*

Beloved, when we strip ourselves of all our guises and window dressing, the raw, innermost hearts of ours, become ready to walk towards God. - *Feb 06, 2011*

Suffering is not a bad thing, if we do not dwell on it and deify it, nor reject its presence in self-denial, but focus only in ways of God. - *Feb 06, 2011*

Beloved, do not believe that our hearts are always safe from the attacks of the evil one, for pride can easily undo the little faith in us. - *Feb 06, 2011*

Each step towards God is a step of our faith meeting God's light and mercy, and never neglect the importance of a single step, ever forward. - *Feb 06, 2011*

Beloved, let us only remember the giant beam in our eyes and on our shoulders, and let us tend to prayer to God, and not the mote in others. - *Feb 06, 2011*

In things harsh and extreme, lies a grave danger of the fracture of the bones of the heart. True faith rests in the gentle rhythm of prayer. - *Feb 06, 2011*

When our hearts are truly healed by the love of Christ, then we are able to find courage, faith, charity and love to be freely given to all. - *Feb 06, 2011*

Hearts after that of Christ, shines with warm light to calm and teach the hearts of many, and not as a flame that hurts and inflames others. - *Feb 06, 2011*

Don't imagine finding solace in the company of man, if you forsake Truth and Love of God. Never compromise or stray from His salvific ways. - *Feb 08, 2011*

Do not feel compelled, inflamed, or depressed over a constantly transient world. God, His Word and love, is infinite and ever constant. - *Feb 08, 2011*

Peace evades those who wage war in deeds or words, but rests within those who love God and others in deeds, words and heart. - *Feb 08, 2011*

Peace can't be stolen through war. Peace begins in the dark recesses of our hearts where we shed our arms, shred our pride, and limp to God. - *Feb 08, 2011*

The erratic ways of the world and the empty promises of the evil one, make the constancy of God and His ways our true pillar and rest. *- Feb 09, 2011*

Beloved, loving others out of faith in God, is not an ecumenical activity. It is the basic tenet of being a Christian, in obedience to God. *- Feb 09, 2011*

One who hates another has already committed murder, of his own soul, and that of another (1 John 3:14-20). Abide in the heart of Christ. *- Feb 09, 2011*

Pray for those close to us who are trapped by the evil one's lures of depression and are sunken in hellish suffering. Lord have mercy. *- Feb 10, 2011*

If one's anger arises even out of a seemingly righteous motive, examine it, drop it quickly. Return to inner prayer; ask for God's mercy. *- Feb 10, 2011*

Do not be misled by the evil one's many guises. Examine all things before the Word of God, and pray with fervor to God for illumination. *- Feb 10, 2011*

Saints come in guises that elude us, while the evil one's many guises are insidious and deceiving. God is our mirror to reveal all things. *- Feb 10, 2011*

Everything God does for oneself, He does it out of love and mercy. God does not favor the rich or powerful. He loves all that He created. *- Feb 10, 2011*

When one denounces God, everything seems to be evil, as if the whole world has wronged him. Conversely, those who find God, find only peace. *- Feb 10, 2011*

Beloved, God transcends all suffering, all pain, all evil. Recognize His face in everything we touch, see, hear, sense, and feel. He is. *- Feb 10, 2011*

Beloved, don't be tempted with lures of quick "spiritual" growth. Look to God's creation in nature – they grow slowly, steadily, silently. *- Feb 11, 2011*

Do not imagine salvation to be assured by anyone, big or small, as sin afflicts all. Be humble, be mindful, be prayerful, and seek only God. *- Feb 12, 2011*

God alone can turn the darkest of sinners and transfigure them into saints. Do not judge, and do not doubt the sovereignty of God in all. *- Feb 12, 2011*

What lens do we see God in? Do we doubt His love for us in many things? Or do we find all of His ways as merciful and loving in shaping us? *- Feb 12, 2011*

The language of God is love. He does all things from love. Do not be deceived by the evil one, who does all out of hatred, for God and all. - *Feb 12, 2011*

Some of us are rich, some not. Some are healthy, some not. Yet, whatever condition we are in, God is tending to us to enrich us towards Him. - *Feb 12, 2011*

Let not the voice of a stranger roaring from the depths of evil erode your faith in God, your trust in Christ, and the Holy Spirit as guide. - *Feb 12, 2011*

Discern through humble prayer, people's voices that call on you – is it of God? Or something else? God speaks truth positively with love. - *Feb 12, 2011*

God intends that every one of us choose happiness, not sadness. We find eternal happiness when we choose Him, and leave all else behind. - *Feb 13, 2011*

If we acknowledge God as our Father, should we not feel safe as we fall snugly back into His loving arms, in all the times of our lives? - *Feb 13, 2011*

Colossal human creations come and go, as we observe the things of the world – transient. The only unshakeable constant here and after? God. - *Feb 13, 2011*

Beloved, may God keep you safe from spiritual dangers; strong in meeting refining challenges; humble in life, and faithful in prayer to Him. *– Feb 13, 2011*

If we imagine we can pick up a stone to stone others, that stone weighs on us heavily, and burns us painfully, for we are but sinners. *– Feb 13, 2011*

Beloved, remember first, God. Remember His love and truth for us through His Word. Remember too, His comfort to us through the Holy Spirit. *– Feb 13, 2011*

The yearning of signs is dangerous for a pilgrim and can be traps by the evil one. Seek only God, through penitent and humble prayer. – Feb 13, 2011

Don't deify oneself or idolize signs and visions for the devil preys on our lust for powers. Look at nothing except unceasing prayer to God. *– Feb 13, 2011*

Just as we don't fast to exhibit righteousness, let us pray and help those in need wherever and whenever the Holy Spirit stirs our hearts. *– Feb 13, 2011*

True awakening to God comes at the expense of self and the passions, and tears at the very fabric of one's heart to be raw for God's flame. *– Feb 14, 2011*

In these days, the dark appears as light, and the light is painted as darkness. Our only compass is God's Truth, and love as the barometer. *– Feb 14, 2011*

In God's creation, we find perfection in its fine balance. We also find God's sense of good humor in some of the wondrous nature. It is joy. - *Feb 14, 2011*

Beloved, when troubled, all we need to do is to step out of our walls, and into God's nature. Breathe in, look around, smell, hear, pray. - *Feb 14, 2011*

Love is difficult for most of us. Charity and kindness perhaps a little easier but not by much. But silent meekness? We can at least try. - *Feb 14, 2011*

Once we label people, we have no love for them. But if we see anyone who comes our way as an icon of Christ, we begin to walk closer to God. - *Feb 14, 2011*

There is a time to be still to wait for God's will and desires. There is a time to be on our feet, to be laboring hard, to be in motion. - *Feb 15, 2011*

God does not reject us, ever. Do not be deceived by anyone who tricks you to believe otherwise. Just walk to God and He is there, all along. - *Feb 15, 2011*

The evil one rejoices when we lose control of ourselves, when we indulge in hatred and anger, often for the little things that don't matter. - *Feb 15, 2011*

Judge not the sins of others, but use that as a reflection of our own and repent earnestly, and humbly pray to God for mercy and providence. – *Feb 16, 2011*

We are to labor as God ordained, earnestly with appreciation. His merciful providence is not a lottery, nor to be exploited, or demanded. – *Feb 17, 2011*

Labor with joy for fruits of earnest labor is sweet indeed. Pray in the heart and call out to Christ, for He is with us in labor or at rest. – *Feb 17, 2011*

Every moment can be a profound moment with God, especially busy ones that can distort our vision. Seek Him in motion and in stillness. – *Feb 17, 2011*

Time is fleeting, and often lost quickly and quietly. Do we lament, or do we seize time by its horns and center it on God and His will? – *Feb 17, 2011*

Before we regret at the end of our journey, let us remember God as we see the constancy of the sunrise, and fulfill our roles dutifully. – *Feb 17, 2011*

The transient nature of modern philosophies and their many errors, only illustrate the full and commanding presence of God's Truth in life. – *Feb 18, 2011*

Beloved, appreciate all the little things around us, and soon we will begin to discern the presence and Truth of God, Who created all things. - *Feb 18, 2011*

God knocks constantly on our doors to no avail. We can try walking towards Him from now on, so that He is mercifully joyous at our attempts. - *Feb 18, 2011*

Our hearts are often in flux, distracted by many things of the world. Know what they are and leave them behind. Give time to God instead. - *Feb 18, 2011*

Before we judge or preach to another, let us help and do good for others instead, so that our generosity speak the truth and love of God. - *Feb 18, 2011*

Beloved, our Christian love is to be able to lay our lives down for others, feed them, clothe them, care for them, and love them as our own. - *Feb 18, 2011*

Dear God, even when I am fallen, of grave sin of my own doing, You are here, with me. Thank You Lord, please lead me safely for I am weak. - *Feb 20, 2011*

We will not find God or His Heaven when we look at others as sinners. Rather, we find His Heaven when we begin to see saints in all we meet. - *Feb 20, 2011*

Beloved, please do not think of any task as menial or meaningless, for every task can be turned into a prayer unto God, a moment with Him. *– Feb 20, 2011*

God gave us life, some long, some short, to use it to the fullest to grow closer to Him. He gave us a place in the world, to pray and love. *– Feb 20, 2011*

God chose His laborers – a mystery, awesome, frightening, and humbling. The priesthood is not merely a vestment occasionally, but for life. *– Feb 20, 2011*

Want lots, and your hearts are often burdened. Want not, and your hearts are light and free. For Christ asked us to focus on and pray unto God. *– Feb 21, 2011*

Life is a Divine jigsaw puzzle and the environment and we are all intricately interwoven into a masterpiece of God. Learn to appreciate all. *– Feb 21, 2011*

Treasure the gift of life, however challenging or transient. You may be amazed at how much you appreciate it if you have faith in God. *– Feb 22, 2011*

God is sovereign, which means He does not struggle against powers that oppose Him. He created all and knows infinity. He is limitless. *– Feb 22, 2011*

Beloved, do not be deceived and deify the evil one and imagine him to be equal to God. God alone is Lord God who is above everything. - *Feb 22, 2011*

Beloved, in all things trust God, no matter how things seem impossible, painful, or even senseless. Rely not on logic, but faith and prayer. - *Feb 22, 2011*

Beloved, God alone will embrace us without expecting much except our love for Him. Conversely, the devil craves only for our destruction. - *Feb 22, 2011*

Behind all cloudy skies is the same unchanging God who shines His brilliant truth and love yearning to nurture all who will walk to Him. - *Feb 22, 2011*

Beloved, be not afraid. The hollowness of a heart is merely a vessel yearning to be filled with humble prayer unto Christ, crying for mercy. - *Feb 22, 2011*

Beloved, be blind to discord that is the devil's work. Priesthood is a Divine mystery, rejoice. Honor and love them as icons of Christ. - *Feb 23, 2011*

What better way for the evil one to destroy faith in God, then to break His servants and to sow discord amongst believers? Discern and pray. - *Feb 23, 2011*

Beloved, do not be entrapped by mirages of the evil one in your pilgrimage across the desert. Pray to God with penance and humility always. – *Feb 24, 2011*

Beloved, even as wonders arise, look beyond them, for our concern is not the existence of God, but simply loving Him with or without signs. – *Feb 24, 2011*

God lends spiritual consolations in our journeys, as transient gifts, not to be indulged upon. As St Paul said, we are soldiers of Christ. – *Feb 24, 2011*

Amidst troubling times, do not let hatred rise to kill your faith in God. For Christ told us not to hate, but to love, even dying to love. – *Feb 24, 2011*

The evil one will always incite us to lust, greed, anger, and hatred. We are to fight his lures and keep returning to prayer of the heart. – *Feb 24, 2011*

Lord Jesus Christ ... Son of God ...... Have mercy on me ... a sinner ...... – *Feb 24, 2011*

We honor Christ when we pray, care for, and love others who are hungry, homeless, ill, and in anguish (inspired by St John Chrysostom). – *Feb 25, 2011*

When sailing through difficult waters, remember that our God shines above, constant, unchanging, ever warm, and that He will guide us home. - *Feb 25, 2011*

Beloved, when we see a wounded man, embrace him like a brother, heal him, feed him, shelter him, and keep him company. That is Christian. - *Feb 25, 2011*

Many things in life can be both weapons, and tools. It is our hearts that determine if we choose them to serve God's purpose, or others. - *Feb 25, 2011*

When our tongues are parched by the heat of our words, it is time for us to let them become moistened and healed by prayer unto God again. - *Feb 26, 2011*

In our secular struggles, Psalm 4:4 says it well, "In your anger do not sin; when you are on your beds, search your hearts and be silent." - *Feb 26, 2011*

Merciful God, thank you for your daily gentle miracles, many of which we were too busy to notice or care for. Yet You were always there. - *Feb 26, 2011*

Beloved, nothing happens by chance. God in His infinite wisdom has knowledge of all things that was, is, and is to come. Rely only on Him. - *Feb 26, 2011*

Lord if I can see no more, in Your mercy, be my vision, and my lantern. When I falter and fall, Lord, be my high tower, shield and sword. – *Feb 26, 2011*

May you be joyous in spirit, eager in learning, humble in prayer, light in heart, kind in action, wondrous in speech, ever closer to God. – *Feb 26, 2011*

May your journey be blessed with abundance of God's mercy and peace, and an abundance of joy in every step, so that you may pass the joy on. – *Feb 26, 2011*

When we have peace and joy, may God grant us diligent labor and prayer. When we falter and tire, may God grant us strength and prayer too. – *Feb 26, 2011*

Beloved, let us marvel at God's creation everyday, for things huge and microscopic lend a beauty to His genius, His sovereignty, His love. – *Feb 26, 2011*

Beloved, do not fear God and walk away from Him, for that is the ploy of the evil one deluding you to walk away. God yearns for you, always. – *Feb 26, 2011*

Beloved, God sends His saints to fill in the gaps in our lives when we falter and are weak at our knees. Praise our Lord God for His mercy. – *Feb 27, 2011*

Life is a journey of ups and downs. Do not give up when there are downs, for the ups will come soon enough, for God never forsakes us. - *Feb 27, 2011*

For when we are weak, God listens to our humble pleas for mercy, and soothes our bruises. God intends that we stand up, and labor onwards. - *Feb 27, 2011*

Beloved, never let your spirit be broken by the curses of the evil one, for if we call unto Christ, He will lend us His infinite strength. - *Feb 27, 2011*

In every new bright morning, beloved, do we get a sense of our God's will and mercy in action again? Do we lean on Him today, yet again? - *Feb 27, 2011*

Dear God, I am moved to tears, that You have gifted me with kind souls along my journey. Grant me strength, and may You bless them always! - *Feb 27, 2011*

Beloved, this morning, the sun shone through dark clouds, with amazing beams of light. This is our God's mercy at work. Pray, beloved. - *Feb 27, 2011*

Our Lord God is merciful, and He lends strength to we who are weak, peace when we are troubled, and love when we are despised. Thank You! - *Feb 28, 2011*

Beloved, let us embrace and receive each and every gift of mercy from God with faith, tears and joy. God surprises us often in simple ways. *- Feb 28, 2011*

Notice how our footsteps vanish behind as we trek through the desert? That reminds us to strip ourselves of prideful egos as we walk to God. *- Feb 28, 2011*

God's love is constant, but His love burns us who are like black coal, and warms us who are like a still pond that sustains life in others. *- Feb 28, 2011*

Beloved, recognize that God fully intends us to find heaven with Him, that we love Him with joyous prayer, and not turn our backs to Him. *- Feb 28, 2011*

Beloved, prayer does not to be confined to a place only. We can pray unto God when we breathe, walk, observe nature, work, and play sports. *- Feb 28, 2011*

Beloved, the way to showing others the Ways of Christ, is simply to provide care and show love for others, and live a life of faith in God. *- Mar 01, 2011*

Beloved, let us with humble loving pleas pray unto God, for those close to us and those we know, whom know not the love of Christ yet. Amen. *- Mar 01, 2011*

Beloved, we soldiers of Christ, let us unite in prayer, steer clear of the passions, remember and care for those in need, as we walk to God. - *Mar 01, 2011*

Beloved, when we go to God with reconciliation, the evil one loses a powerful weapon used to wedge between God and us - our prideful egos. - *Mar 02, 2011*

Beloved, God hears all our prayers, especially those we pray earnestly for others facing difficulties. In all things, abide in His time. - *Mar 03, 2011*

Beloved, when we are dragged about in a hurried day with hardly time to breathe, it is time to pause a little, to pray the Jesus Prayer. - *Mar 04, 2011*

Beloved, only when we slow down, especially to stillness, can we yet again hear God. Find our closet wherever we are to pray, in silence. - *Mar 04, 2011*

Beloved, it is all right to put aside a roadblock if we are without immediate answers, for we can leave our obstacles with God. Let us pray. - *Mar 04, 2011*

Beloved, while we remember to care for little ones and small animals, consider also the aged, for their twilight should not impede our love. - *Mar 04, 2011*

Every person in need becomes yet another step for us forward towards God, when we stretch out our hands to serve and care for the needs. - *Mar 04, 2011*

Lord Jesus Christ... Son of God...... Have mercy on me... a sinner...... - *Mar 06, 2011*

When we no longer regard others as enemies, and with humble and repentant prayer unto God, we begin our healing journey back to God. - *Mar 06, 2011*

"Avoid the wave of evil. Get to know and study the spirit of the times to avoid its influence whenever possible." St Ignatius Brianchaninov. - *Mar 06, 2011*

Beloved, when we suffer great pain and shoulder heavy burdens, cry unto God with all our heart, and He will tend to us with Divine healing. - *Mar 07, 2011*

It is not hard to discern things of evil. The question is, are we actually willing to let them go, repent and go back to God with prayer? - *Mar 08, 2011*

Beloved, be wary of a restless condition, as it stirs us to approach the passions. Return to the penitent prayer of the heart for stillness. - *Mar 08, 2011*

Beloved, please remember our faith is labor. We labor in love and faith in God, and seek no fruits except a rest in Him. Let us pray. - *Mar 08, 2011*

Beloved, do not drown out our inner emptiness with burdens of work or play. Instead, fill such a void with prayer and praises unto God. - *Mar 08, 2011*

Beloved, we are not alone especially when we pray for the sake of others with faith, for our Theotokos and holy saints pray with us also. - *Mar 08, 2011*

Fear not things in our path except our own fallen hearts, for they are often our greatest enemies. In all things lean on God with prayer. - *Mar 10, 2011*

Nothing like being close to the ground to realize how far removed we are from God. In our daily labors, let us pray and grow closer to Him. - *Mar 10, 2011*

Lord have mercy; lend us Your strength and kindness to help all in need; lend us Your Truth and grace to turn all to You in faithful prayer. - *Mar 11, 2011*

Dear God, let us never depart from You with fear of dangers and challenges, lend us Your mercy to only follow Your path of light and love. - *Mar 11, 2011*

Life is a wondrous journey with God, provided we become blind to bias and hatred, and learn to grow in the Ways and Word of God every day. - *Mar 12, 2011*

Beloved, do we even know how long we have? How our lives will be? It does not matter as long as we keep our sights and trust only in God. - *Mar 12, 2011*

Beloved, always pray for the faithful, but also love all so that others can find solace in God too, through our words, deeds and prayers. - *Mar 13, 2011*

There is nothing more illuminating and evangelizing in the life of a Christian than one whom selflessly gives care, prayers and love to all. - *Mar 14, 2011*

Beloved, what if one were to have eternity? What would one do? What is the purpose? What would drive one from here to eternity? Think, pray. - *Mar 15, 2011*

There is no "I" in "Heaven", because that is the abode of "He", our Lord and God, where His mercy allows some to be with Him eternally. - *Mar 15, 2011*

Be mighty in charity, but shy in enjoyment; be courageous in faith, but naught in passions; be strong in prayer, but dim in judgment. - *Mar 15, 2011*

May we be a ray of light, not of flames; a book of truth, not of judgment; a dose of healing, not of pain; a beacon of love, not of hurt. - *Mar 17, 2011*

Lord, have mercy when we crawl through the scorching sands of the desert, and grant us strength to pray unto You, and find rest beyond. - *Mar 20, 2011*

Even a single drop of God's mercy can propel us forward, despite a broken body and exhausted soul, if only we abandon our pride and doubts. - *Mar 22, 2011*

There's a rhythm in life if we slow down, listen with discernment and humble prayer unto God. Realize that and you sense His mercy with you. - *Mar 22, 2011*

St. John the Beloved leaned on Christ and listened to His heartbeat, a deep resonating rhythm of eternity and a vastness of loving Truth. - *Mar 22, 2011*

When we pray the prayer of the heart, we begin to feel simultaneously tears of remorse of sins, smiles of relief and freedom in God's mercy. - *Mar 22, 2011*

Beloved, in every roadblock, never lose hope, for Christ is with us all the way as long as we abandon all but prayer, faith and love. - *Mar 22, 2011*

There is Divine reason why we who are in the world, are in the world. Work with God's will, not against. In all things, faith and charity. - *Mar 23, 2011*

Beloved, be wary of the lure of wealth, for it can corrupt our souls insidiously. Discern, use it wisely, give it lovingly, and pray humbly. - *Mar 24, 2011*

When someone comes to us for spiritual matters, it is us who receives a gift from God to pray even more with discipline, humility and faith. - *Mar 24, 2011*

We don't enter Heaven by enjoyment, but with our passions torn away, our sins charred, and we look only to God with just faith and prayer. - *Mar 24, 2011*

The devil tries his every might to delude us that God doesn't measure up, doesn't exist, or doesn't care. Disbelieve every such suggestion. - *Mar 24, 2011*

Beloved, pray for clergy and their burdens for the yoke of Christ, for the evil one will do anything and use anyone to erase priesthood. - *Mar 24, 2011*

Beloved, do not curse any condition we confront, for every condition can be our stepping stone towards God, so long as we look only to Him. - *Mar 26, 2011*

Beloved, even with degenerating sight viewing a blurred world, I know and experience the empowering, pervasive love and mercy of God within. - *Mar 26, 2011*

Beloved, remember the Cross of Christ, and His Resurrection. May we receive the dew of His salvific love as we trek through our desert. - *Mar 26, 2011*

There's something beautiful about silence. It allows us to realize the calmness and allow our ears to be able to humbly discern Divine Will. - *Mar 26, 2011*

When we begin to bring our attention to inner prayer unto God, to discern, the noises and distractions around us begin to melt away. - *Mar 26, 2011*

Often, we are in a needless tug-of-war with God, contesting our feeble wills with Divine Will. Instead, trust God in His providential mercy. - *Mar 27, 2011*

God is infinite joy, and all we need to be convinced of that, is simply to look at the beauty of nature He masterfully and lovingly created. - *Mar 27, 2011*

Against spiritual dangers and exhaustion, remember the Holy Name of Jesus Christ, whose light exposes all darkness and melts all sorrow. - *Mar 27, 2011*

The "sweetness" of the fruits of evil seems hollow, while the sweetness of walking towards God is one of tears of joy, heart of contentment. - *Mar 27, 2011*

Christ our Lord whom we profess our faith and love, taught us not to damn, but to care; not to hurt, but to heal; not to idle, but to pray. - *Mar 27, 2011*

Look pass mere words, but look into the deeds and hearts, for all saints showed us their holy hearts and mighty deeds, amidst few words. - *Mar 29, 2011*

If we are reduced to nothing, pray the prayer of the heart, because we call the Holy Name of Jesus Christ, and ask for mercy for our sins. - *Mar 29, 2011*

If a tongue indulges in the passion of war, it becomes exhausted, weak in the calm joy of inner prayer calling the Name of Christ for mercy. - *Mar 30, 2011*

If a brother becomes weak, lift him up. If he becomes hurt, cure his wounds. If he turns wrongly, embrace him and walk with him to the Lord. - *Mar 30, 2011*

Seek no revenge, for the devil wants us to sink into passions of anger and hatred. Instead, pray, go silent, asking for God's mercy for all. - *Mar 30, 2011*

Seek only the Kingdom of God, pray for the mercy of Christ, for all worldly things are unimportant compared to an eternity to endure. - *Mar 30, 2011*

The devil works through humans who bend to his lures of malice, even in the name of Christ. Ignore all such flames, pray, and seek only God. - *Mar 30, 2011*

Weigh all things through the lens of Scripture and the Fathers, and humbled prayer, and discern if we see hatred, or the love of Christ. - *Mar 30, 2011*

Do not sway to flames of noise in the world, but be steadfast in prayer as a cornerstone, and pliable like a blade of grass, in His mercy. - *Mar 30, 2011*

If we cannot even love others as ourselves whom we can see, how can we love God Whom we cannot see? (St John of Kronstadt) - *Mar 30, 2011*

If you are angry against your neighbor, you are angry against God. If you revile a man, you revile the image of God (St Ephraim the Syrian). - *Mar 30, 2011*

God's Truth, like the sun, shines universally and pervasively with the loving intent to nurture all who are willing, and bring them life. - *Mar 31, 2011*

A saint is akin to reflective glass, pristine and permeable to the light of God, and reflective in communion with God through humble faith. - *Mar 31, 2011*

Repentant prayer unto God, a conscious effort, is like a searing fire that transfigures our pains from sin into a blissful state of warmth. - *Mar 31, 2011*

Arrogance hardens the heart, renders it opaque to the mercy and love of God; while humility expands and softens the heart, making it God's. - *Mar 31, 2011*

If there seems anything that raises our passions, relieve such burdens, which impede our walk towards God, unto the Lord in humble prayer. - *Mar 31, 2011*

Seek nothing, except God's mercy for us to pray unceasingly, even as the devil tries to tear our feeble prayers apart, for God is strength. - *Mar 31, 2011*

Prayer from the lips and the mind can cease. When prayer with utmost humility becomes breathing and the heart beating, it is unceasing. - *Mar 31, 2011*

God makes no mistakes. It is up to us to talk with God, to understand what He intends with us, and how we transform our lives towards Him. - *Mar 31, 2011*

Beloved, in all things, wait for the Lord, for He alone has seen our whole lives from beginning to end. We only need to pray, and love all. - *Apr 01, 2011*

The ascent towards God becomes a joy when we realize how much He supported us from behind, and that His light of love shines on us all over. - *Apr 01, 2011*

We are made to pilgrim to God in a limited time, however long or short, for a time of eternity. That eternity of life, or death is up to us. - *Apr 01, 2011*

Beloved, do not be blind to all the beauty of subtle signs God has carefully placed along our journey. This journey is special, made by God. - *Apr 01, 2011*

Beloved, at the end of the journey, however long or short, we will be measured on how much we love God, and love others, nothing else. - *Apr 04, 2011*

A true saint is one whose heart has bled dry of passions and hatred, and filled with love for God, for His children, with prayer and deeds. – *Apr 04, 2011*

Beloved, we are called to be Christian soldiers, fighting the passions within us. We are called to be marathoners, to complete the journey. – *Apr 04, 2011*

When the voice of evil rises against us, let us keep silent, but be diligent in prayer unto God, for God is the final arbiter, not mere men. – *Apr 04, 2011*

Distinguish Christianity not by people of ecclesiastical titles, but by the Truth and by the exactness of the Faith – St Gregory Palamas. – *Apr 04, 2011*

Take a deep breath when work drowns us, walk away from the desk, stretch a bit, and pray the Jesus Prayer. Every break can be prayer time. – *Apr 04, 2011*

The trials we face are to strengthen us, not to weaken or break us. What we need is to humble ourselves and leave our burdens with God. – *Apr 04, 2011*

Beloved, let us use the yardstick of Proverbs 15 to measure our daily speech, especially to bring joy to others, and honor God Whom we love. – *Apr 05, 2011*

The fruit of the devil is hatred while that of the Holy Spirit is joy. So pray for God's mercy, that all we say and do is filled with joy. - *Apr 06, 2011*

Pray unto God, that we die to the world, and live in Him. We find our burdens lifted when we live in Him, our hearts free to care and love. - *Apr 06, 2011*

When confronted with challenges, never allow anyone to bring our spirituality, our faith in God, to its knees. God is our pillar and summit. - *Apr 06, 2011*

The more we hurt others, the darker we feel. The more we love others above our own needs, the more we begin to truly feel the love of God. - *Apr 06, 2011*

Prelest can overcome even the most pious, when our inner greed for signs overtakes our honest and simple life of penitent prayer unto God. - *Apr 06, 2011*

Beloved, remember our faith and love for God, that it has always been an inner and sacred journey shared between God and us. - *Apr 06, 2011*

Beloved, we are asked to endure, for that brings us close to God in His salvific love. Do not retreat from Him. Pray for strength in Him. - *Apr 06, 2011*

Civility is a mark of faith that allows one not to fear the unknown or the dreaded, but to stand firm in God, and extending warmth to all. *- Apr 07, 2011*

God has ordained some in deep suffering and yet triumphantly joyous, to nourish our spirits to continue. Never give up! Lean on His mercy. *- Apr 07, 2011*

Even a meeting can be finding the Lord. Speak constructively, respectfully, succinctly. When all else, listen well, and pray in between. *- Apr 07, 2011*

Beloved, do not get caught up with anything in the world, except God who humbles us, He who strengthens us, He who mercifully forgives us. *- Apr 08, 2011*

Remember our most beloved Theotokos, who is always listening. Our Theotokos, pray for us for Christ our Lord, in our hours of fatigue. *- Apr 08, 2011*

Beloved, never doubt that Christ can abide in anyone, and that everyone has been lovingly created by God. What could we do but to love all? *- Apr 09, 2011*

The rain can nourish, or destroy; much depends on the condition of the soil it falls on. Likewise, what would God's loving light mean to us? *- Apr 09, 2011*

The greatest miracle of God is that Christ is with us. He tends to us in loving mercy, profound light of truth, everyday we walk with Him. - *Apr 09, 2011*

Beloved, the Holy Name of Jesus Christ our Lord, asking His mercy at all times, is the pure light that dispels all fears, evil, weaknesses. - *Apr 09, 2011*

A priest may experience many different things in a day, birth, sickness, death, marriage, etc. God lends His mercy and strength to us all. - *Apr 10, 2011*

For every hurtful person who crosses our paths, imagine their own hurts and inner hell. Comfort them, bless them, edify them, pray for them. - *Apr 10, 2011*

If we feel cold and shattered in a corner, remember it will be a moment in time - transient. God is sovereign, leave the burden with Him. - *Apr 11, 2011*

The Lord our God hears us when our feeble voices call unto Him. If the journey is long and arduous, do not give up for He is near. - *Apr 11, 2011*

Never forsake that which seems hard to us - confession, for it is the Holy Mystery that reunites us back with God Who hears our cries. - *Apr 11, 2011*

Age, power and wealth do not make us any better than another. Humility, faith and love are what draw us ever closer to God, nearer to all. – *Apr 11, 2011*

Pride can lead us to deify falsehood and ourselves, that we may be blinded from seeing and touching the gentle warmth and truth of Christ. – *Apr 12, 2011*

Beloved, pride may be the most dangerous passion, for it can delude us to think we are rooted in faith and Truth, the precursor to prelest. – *Apr 12, 2011*

Beloved, when we judge the spiritual disfigurement of another, we have exposed the raw and decaying sores of our own such disfigurement. – *Apr 13, 2011*

The beginning of theosis is the ending of our lust after passions. The opening of our hearts to God is the closing of our dwelling in pride. – *Apr 14, 2011*

Suffering is part of the mystery of life. Does such suffering lean us closer to God, or do we choose destructive depression away from God? – *Apr 14, 2011*

The mystery of our spiritual journey demands much from a humbled heart in deep prayer, so that God lends His strength to us to brave on. - *Apr 14, 2011*

Sometimes God demands us to rise up to His call and not be weak. We can only pray fervently unto Him to light our paths, to be ever closer. - *Apr 15, 2011*

God, lend me strength as You demand that I stand and do Your work. I have no excuse if I profess faith in Your providential might and will. - *Apr 15, 2011*

Christ my Lord, grant me mercy that I can also hear your heartbeat that resonated the heart and soul of St John when he leaned on you. - *Apr 15, 2011*

Christ's heartbeat is one of constancy, firmness, and assurance, where one can experience only in the most silent and humble of prayers. - *Apr 15, 2011*

Beloved, the pilgrimage is not a project, measured by worldly deliverables, but one of rooted faith, trusting God, bountiful in prayer. - *Apr 15, 2011*

Ever closer our Christ draws near to us, beloved, do not depart, nor retreat from Him. Let Him heal our wounds, unto ages of ages. Amen. - *Apr 16, 2011*

Look beyond mere words, beloved, but discern if they spring from labors and hearts of love, or merely of judgment and self-righteousness. - *Apr 17, 2011*

To speak is easy, but to labor, hard. Those who do must foremost, be doers of His Word, givers of His love, and listeners of His people. - *Apr 17, 2011*

When we lay down during our ordination, with tears, we lay down our lives for Christ, for His work, and for His people, in faith and love. - *Apr 17, 2011*

Beloved, when we see someone in need, someone who thinks different from us, offer an olive branch and nourishment, not wield a battle-axe. - *Apr 17, 2011*

Even to our last breath we wrestle with our own prideful passions and their lures of death. Fight back with confession, discernment, prayer. - *Apr 17, 2011*

Do not compare your life with another, if you trust the Lord and His Will, for He knows you, and lovingly created each for a unique journey. - *Apr 18, 2011*

Every one of us is a work of art by God. No one is identical to another in their journey of life, not even twins. Treasure God's art in us. - *Apr 18, 2011*

The ground is soft when your steps are gentle. The light is warm when your heart is humble. The air is sweet when your tongue is edifying. *- Apr 18, 2011*

Beloved, may we pray with tears unto God today, asking for His mercy for all our passions and sins, that we may be rendered whole for Him. *- Apr 19, 2011*

Beloved, do not show Christ the back of our heads, denying His love. But let us face Christ, so our sins and burdens are laid before Him. *- Apr 21, 2011*

Christ asked us to carry our crosses and follow Him, out of a willing sacrifice, of love for God and others. It's possible only through God. *- Apr 21, 2011*

Faith in God is not when it seems all things are well, but especially when we face a deep loss and a grave hurt, and accepting it like Job. *- Apr 22, 2011*

Are we trapped by issues that retard our faith towards God? Are we spending time squabbling, judging, procrastinating, rather than praying? *- Apr 23, 2011*

We spend 7 hours resting, 3 hours commuting, 8 hours working, 2 hours eating, 1 hour on chores, and we have just 3 precious hours left for? *- Apr 23, 2011*

Christ wanted us not just to remember the cross we bear with Him daily as His, but especially of the life ever after when He conquered death. - *Apr 23, 2011*

The evil one distorts our sense of reality, by manipulating our exhaustion. Ignore these distractions, and continue our gaze unto God. - *Apr 24, 2011*

The fruit of the vine of humble and penitent prayer is not abundance as we imagine it, but rather, the mercy to carry on loving God and all. - *Apr 25, 2011*

God has infinite patience as is His love and mercy. He keeps knocking on our doors despite us hiding away from Him. For how long do we hide? - *Apr 25, 2011*

God knows as well as we do that we are at home. Why not simply invite Him to live with us forever? There will be changes, all good ones. - *Apr 25, 2011*

Even if we can recite thousands of verses from Scripture and Patristic texts, At the end, God will ask us, "Have you loved Me. and others?" - *Apr 25, 2011*

Do not think lightly of your expressions. Your negativity can cause dejection in your brethren. Your joy and smile, lighten their burdens. - *Apr 25, 2011*

God does not discriminate us if we are poor. He cares if we worship Him with the intensity, solemnity, and discipline of true love for Him. - *Apr 26, 2011*

Let us always shut out the noises of distraction, for God calls us to be His, and our marathon in life is to be running to Him. - *Apr 28, 2011*

Mortals show their true colors if provoked and acting out of self-interest. Saints show their true colors even when harassed beyond belief. - *Apr 28, 2011*

If a holy icon drops into a lake we will dive in to save it even in freezing water. Wouldn't that apply to the living, all images of Christ? - *Apr 28, 2011*

Let the Resurrection of Christ in Holy Pascha remind what His Message and Instruction to us who profess faith in Him truly is – love. - *Apr 28, 2011*

Remember St Thomas who first professed, "My Lord and my God!" Pray for the dearly reposed. Christ is Risen! Truly He is Risen! Peace to all! - *Apr 29, 2011*

If you sign a contract of death with the devil, any fruition, however glamorous it seems, will only end in disappointment and death. *- Apr 30, 2011*

The beginning of anger, the culmination in hatred, is the progress towards spiritual death. God did not say love your enemies when you want. *- May 02, 2011*

Remember whose side we are asked to be on, Christ, or those who wanted to stone someone. What is our faith, if it is merely to judge others? *- May 03, 2011*

True compassion challenges our hearts to such depths, because it demands and wrestles our own needs away, and places needs of others first. *- May 03, 2011*

Lord have mercy on my soul, for I have many sins. Grant me Thy mercy and do not leave me, for the challenges are great and my heart small. *- May 03, 2011*

God loves all His creation. We are not His judges, nor His executioners. We are told to be His laborers to love all His creation and Him. *- May 03, 2011*

No one deserves to be hated, just as much as none of us deserve the love and mercy of God. When God loves all, He expects us to do no less. *- May 04, 2011*

What fuels your faith? Is it anger or hatred? Or humility, prayer, and love, which are the signs of abiding in God as He abides in us. - *May 04, 2011*

Do not be misled, beloved, that any amount of hatred can lead to faith in God. It does not. Christ showed us exactly how – faith, and love. - *May 04, 2011*

When you are presented with the road to death that is easy and enjoyable, or the road to life that is arduous and painful, consider wisely. - *May 04, 2011*

If someone comes to me with nothing but his heart, I would see him as a loved one, rather than one who comes with everything but his heart. - *May 05, 2011*

"He who does not love his brother whom he has seen, how can he love God whom he has not seen?" – 1 John 4:20 - *May 05, 2011*

Life is an ever unfolding of seasons, transient and fleeting. And yet we find the constant with every dawn and every moonlit night – God. - *May 09, 2011*

I know that God has already walked my path ahead of me as I seek Him. I only need to pray unto Him to find the subtle signs He left for me. - *May 10, 2011*

Find God's tender mercy and constant love, in the occasional rain in the scorching summer, and the morning sun in the freezing winter. *– May 10, 2011*

It is insufficient to feel an aching pain for the plight of the suffering ones, for we are called to labor with our hands and feet for them. *– May 11, 2011*

Heaven or hell depends much on what or whom we place our faith in and how much we devote to it, in the same situations calling our actions. *– May 11, 2011*

Trust not in the words of princes, but the Word, our Christ. Trust not in the passions of mortals, but the Love of God and His tender mercy. *– May 12, 2011*

Christ came in a simple form, and taught us never to judge others physically. Never be misled by glittering glamor, or despising the meek. *– May 12, 2011*

We are not heroes nor saints, but mere mortals. With God's mercy, we can perhaps walk as far as our faith, prayers, and love can go. *– May 12, 2011*

Beloved, let not our meandering towards many passions be habit forming. Let our habit be only our constant struggles and pilgrimage to God. *– May 15, 2011*

It is the labor we put in for our pilgrimage towards God that is important. We will try, we will falter and fail, and we will try again. *- May 18, 2011*

If we meet Christ with humility and love in every step, every deed, every meeting, we will also meet Him at the last stop of our journey. *- May 22, 2011*

Lift up our hearts in prayer unto God, for He rules over all, with only love and mercy. Let us tread gingerly and let Him be our strength. *- May 23, 2011*

Let not our days of need be the seeds of despair the evil one wields craftily against us; but the tools to strengthen us in prayer unto God. *- May 31, 2011*

There are many bus stops along our journey of life to God. Just remember not to stop or be distracted, and keep going to God at the end. *- May 31, 2011*

In the gravity of sins that drag us down, it is only the lightness of the Holy Strength and Mercy of God, that lift us up and towards Him. *- Jun 05, 2011*

Beloved, there is nothing that God cannot change for our good, as long as we have Him as the sole reason and sustenance of our lives. *- Jun 10, 2011*

If we marvel at God's love for us even in the darkest hours, He is with us. But if we lament over those hours, we have walked away from Him. - *Jun 14, 2011*

To pray penitently unto God for our sins, and to pray for the salvation of others whom we love or do not know yet, brings us closer to God. - *Jun 14, 2011*

Allow the mercy of God to illumine us when we reflect on His Word and holy writings, and disengage our prideful intellect from interfering. - *Jun 17, 2011*

God forgives us by His undying love and unfathomable sacrifices for us despite our frequent failings. What is our forgiveness for others? - *Jun 17, 2011*

Our faith is not a business, but the gathering of the faithful who profess their journeys towards God in prayer, in abandonment of passions. - *Jun 17, 2011*

Sinners and saints alike, can reveal much of God's Mercy through everyday journeys of faith, or wonderworking for the salvation of people. - *Jun 21, 2011*

Let the strength of God shelter us from our passions; let His mercy clothe us with our penitence; let His love warm us with prayer unto Him. *– Jun 26, 2011*

Beloved, let not the fear of reconciliation with our God prevent us from confessing our sins and relieving our burdens unto Him. *– Jun 29, 2011*

To those with wounded egos, let us extend our kinship like a humble child. To those who need our help, let us be like patient fathers. *– Jul 03, 2011*

Be oppressed, rather than the oppressor. Be gentle, rather than zealous. Lay hold of goodness, rather than justice. St. Isaac of Syria. *– Jul 04, 2011*

Beloved, let us pray to God, that our hearts remain tender to the cries, warm to the cold, earnest to those seeking, strong to the faithful. *– Jul 09, 2011*

Justice belongs to God. We are called by Christ Whom we profess as our Lord, to strive for humility, prayer, charity, labor, and love. *– Jul 13, 2011*

Let not mere eloquence seduce us, but the painful labors springing from the love of God and all His creation persuade us to do the same. *– Jul 13, 2011*

Pride begets contempt and hatred not only for others, but deeper yet, a hatred of oneself. The cure is God's gift of humility and penance. – *Jul 13, 2011*

The illumination and warmth of God's true mercy and love can only permeate through our lives when the frail veil of our ego is removed. – *Jul 14, 2011*

Let not voices of any, however presented, dissuade you from your faith for God. Soldier on when you are ridiculed, with love and prayer. – *Jul 14, 2011*

In the beautiful harmony of God's creation we see Him as peace, order, abundance and love. What do we seek when we profess our faith in Him? – *Jul 14, 2011*

"All condemnation is from the devil. Never condemn another, not even those whom you catch committing an evil deed." (St Seraphim of Sarov) – *Jul 14, 2011*

Let not the disfiguring illness we shoulder mask the reality that God has always loved us, still love us, and we are to strive towards Him. – *Jul 14, 2011*

God Who created all made all beautiful in His sight. We strayed from Him, and find things heinous. Restore our sight by walking back to Him. – *Jul 18, 2011*

Beloved, amidst our labors daily, if we spend time to pray for the needs of the young, the old, and all, would we still have time to do ill? – *Jul 21, 2011*

Beloved, we who are called to be in the world laboring away, let us labor in joy, for it is His will we abide, and a prayer when we toil. – *Jul 21, 2011*

Beloved, pride blinds us to how fragile our faith can be. Flush pride out with a strong pint of humility and rely only on the Will of God. – *Jul 21, 2011*

Shed the fanciful garments of pride, oft ill-disguised in many forms, and return to the bare and humbled being, uttering Christ our Lord. – *Jul 22, 2011*

When hands become quick and mindless with hurling stones, they betray a heart sore and wounded. Embrace such a heart with prayerful love. – *Jul 27, 2011*

When we stray from God, He knows our pains due to lust, but does not satiate our wants. He longs for us to simply return to Him with prayer. – *Jul 27, 2011*

The ache in our hearts melts away when we shed these burdens of pride and recognize our frailty, kneels before God, embracing His mercy. - *Aug 01, 2011*

My most holy beloved Theotokos, look to me with loving tears and a mother's love, pray for me, a sinner, unto Christ our Lord and God. - *Aug 01, 2011*

God rewards us who are striving for patience, humility, courage, faith and love, even as we falter in these journeys. Remember, brave on. - *Aug 01, 2011*

Fear belies pride, however meek it seems, for it betrays a lack of faith in God and His Will. Trust in His mercy that can only be from love. - *Aug 02, 2011*

Our Lord and Christ illumines always, and earnestly and lovingly awaits our slow and haphazard ascent up the mount of life and faith to Him. - *Aug 05, 2011*

Love the hands of toil and sweat, for they show the embrace of God's Will for us. A day of labor is sweet prayer as we wipe our brows. - *Aug 05, 2011*

God is always ready to give us a lift to our exhausted bodies and spirits, as long as we are willing to cry to Him in repentance and prayer. - *Aug 05, 2011*

The sign of the Cross is our profession of faith, our protection, our declaration of freedom from the world, and our quiet prayer unto God. - *Aug 11, 2011*

Our Mother, most Holy Theotokos, thank you for your tears of joy as you intercede for we the faithful, even as we pray with tears unto God. - *Aug 14, 2011*

Beloved, the road gets narrower and tougher, but know that God, His angels, His saints, are always silently and subtly along with us. Pray. - *Aug 14, 2011*

God created everything, and everything is good in His eyes. What do our hearts say to all we see, touch, and hear? (insp. by 1 Tim 4:4–5) - *Aug 14, 2011*

There is no faith in God with a sword, for Christ showed us the mystery behind Theosis by His ultimate sacrifice and calling us to the same. - *Aug 16, 2011*

Apathy puts us at the fringe of a frail belief. Hatred sucks us into the epicenter of the devil's abode. Only selfless love walks us to God. - *Aug 17, 2011*

For the darkness of this world rules and blinds many, while those with ears hear. But the true reward is for us who persist till the end. - *Aug 19, 2011*

Often when we fall, remember God lends appropriate strength when we ask of Him, not more, not less, but sufficient in our spiritual growth. - *Aug 21, 2011*

How often, how close are we, to when we are fools for Christ, respecting each person in our paths, as icons, and our Lord's loved creations? - *Aug 21, 2011*

Beloved, what do we see in the still lake, of our own reflection, and what we see of others in the lake? Do we find monstrosity, or icons? - *Aug 22, 2011*

God's eyes are moistened with tears: Of mercy when we turn away from Him to embrace evil; but of joy when we repent and pray unto Him. - *Aug 22, 2011*

When we are blinded by the devil, everything is dark and ugly to our pride. When we are illumined towards God, everything is a blessed art. - *Aug 22, 2011*

The eye of the needle is so small to thread through, that it is not for us to dwell on. Rather, watch if our burdens are given to our Lord. - *Aug 23, 2011*

Just as there were those with humble beginnings were ordained by God to do great things, never judge another as "small" or "insignificant". - *Aug 24, 2011*

The devil patiently wears us out until only anger, bitterness, and desolation is left. Do not let him, but call on the Holy Name of Christ. - *Aug 24, 2011*

Even if many desert God, do not feel lost. The tears of the prayer of our Theotokos and the radiant warmth of our Christ will strengthen us. - *Aug 26, 2011*

Beloved, do not allow the lure of the evil one to delude our growth towards God, especially when all feels dark and hollow. Keep braving on. - *Aug 26, 2011*

When we are sore from the wounds of our sins, do not be afraid. This is when we are given the gift of reconciliation with God. Trust Him. - *Aug 29, 2011*

If we cannot love those who listened to God's call to vocation, can we truly love another, or an "enemy"? Pray for, and love His laborers. - *Aug 29, 2011*

We are not called to think we are right, but to be brave, trusting in the Divine Will and Grace of our Lord. Only our Lord is right, always. - *Aug 31, 2011*

God brings people in our lives, and spurs us to grow towards Him through them. Hate no one, even if they seem to hurt us. Find grace in all. - *Sep 03, 2011*

Beloved, never be lured by the easy descent to the depths of pain, just as never be dissuaded from the ascent on the high mountain of faith. *- Sep 03, 2011*

While the devil tempts us with enjoyment like a glib conman, God is the perspiring blacksmith who moulds us in consuming love towards Him. *- Sep 04, 2011*

Walk gingerly behind the trail of our Christ, tend to the needs and prayers of all who converge with our journey. God will take care of us. *- Sep 07, 2011*

Does one put oneself above all, even above God? Or do we consider ourselves the least of all creatures as St Tithoes of the Thebaid said? *- Sep 08, 2011*

The single word God hopes to hear from us, is "Yes!" while the single word to describe God's response to us for our entire life, is LOVE. *- Sep 12, 2011*

God is always present in the desert as much as He is in the busy city, in silence and in noise. We begin to see and hear Him, when we pray. *- Sep 12, 2011*

Let nothing, nothing, ever stop you short at celebrating life – which is a gift from God. Let no calamity nor sadness overcome you in life. - *Sep 12, 2011*

Each of us who professes and bears the Cross, sees not prideful suffering, but yearns for the dance of joy and the illumination of our Lord. - *Sep 12, 2011*

Let us carry the Torch of the Truth of God to warm fireplaces, light lanterns and candles, and to be a tiny beacon in the dark roads ahead. - *Sep 14, 2011*

There is no gift greater than life that God has gifted us, that it demands that we spend all the time we have to nurture it, to defend it. - *Sep 14, 2011*

The evil one hopes only for our desolation and damnation. God offers only Light and Love, and wants only our salvation and Theosis. - *Sep 15, 2011*

God grants us the gift of innocent wonder, a gift that allows us to marvel at all His creations, and to humbly and joyously walk to Him. - *Sep 15, 2011*

We only begin to have disdain for others when we forsake the gift of innocence from God, and shoulder our will and pride above His Will. - *Sep 19, 2011*

We do not hurt a brother who is fragile and hurt. We are only to embrace him with tenderness and prayers. All wounds need no more injury. - *Sep 19, 2011*

Even if evil stares us down with threats, lies and seduction, keep vigil with only prayers unto God's mercy. Let no negative emotion arise. - *Sep 20, 2011*

Discern and not simply bend to signs and wonders. Bend instead to the Will of God, however plain or even difficult it is against our wills. - *Sep 20, 2011*

The journey is long and the mountain is high, beloved, so travel light with only necessities, constant prayers, and our sights unto God. - *Sep 21, 2011*

God often shows His mercy in subtlety and tenderness, while the evil one often presents his temptations in great drama and fanfare. - *Sep 23, 2011*

God is never absent, contrary to what some might imagine. God's "absence" is merely our own darkness blinding our sights, crippling us. - *Sep 26, 2011*

God may not be found in mechanistic displays, but in a long, arduous pilgrimage of torn skin, broken bones, sweat and tears. Faith is brave. - *Sep 26, 2011*

Those who intend to hurt us have already been hurt and wounded inside. It is not for us to retort or injure them, but to pray for them. - *Sep 26, 2011*

The devil appeals to our pride to delude us to self-righteousness. Our defense? "Lord Jesus Christ, Son of God, have mercy on me, a sinner." - *Sep 28, 2011*

Christ did not show us luxury, fame or titles, but the cross. He called us to simplicity, purity, humility, sacrificial love, and prayer. - *Sep 29, 2011*

There is a time for everything. Fight against laziness when praying. Fight against indulgence for all else, such as labor, rest and leisure. - *Sep 29, 2011*

Christ descended so that we may ascend back to God and never taste hatred again. Do not indulge in the devil's lair where hatred is key. - *Oct 05, 2011*

Do not lament when the world passes us by, nor be proud if we seem to pass before others; for the only pace in life and all belongs to God. - *Oct 05, 2011*

For our Christ and His holy apostles told us, to be kind, forgiving, and tenderhearted to others. What is tenderness? A gentle caring touch. - *Oct 05, 2011*

God seems hidden from us not because He hides from us, but rather, we hide from His light, His truth, and His love. God does not hide, ever. - *Oct 10, 2011*

Look around us, beloved, where is God? He is as close to us as the air we breathe, the warmth of the sun, and the water that nourishes us. - *Oct 10, 2011*

Beloved, treasure the special spiritual friends God sends as gifts to us. They strengthen, encourage, and pray for us. Pray for them always. - *Oct 10, 2011*

The Lord presents saints who inspire us to strengthen our faith unto Him, to pray joyously, to live in peace and love for all His creation. - *Oct 15, 2011*

God knows our hearts, and so, do nothing to rebuke others when we are accused, but submit to humility, for humility is prayer unto God. - *Oct 15, 2011*

Beloved, never imagine God shuts His doors to us. He does not. It is often us who shuts our own doors to His love and mercy. Open our doors. - *Oct 15, 2011*

The body is a unique gift from God, with God's specific love for each one of us. Unravel this mystery through constant and humble prayers. - *Oct 18, 2011*

God does not make mistakes or design flaws. He has a specific Reason for everyone and everything. Dwell not on rants, but prayers unto Him. - *Oct 19, 2011*

Rejoice that we still can pray unto God, however plain our prayers are. Let our pleas for the salvation of others drive our prayers to God. - *Oct 19, 2011*

Our Most Holy Theotokos is a Gift from God, to show us what He wishes for all His children, to be faithful, prayerful, and trusting in Him. - *Oct 19, 2011*

Beloved, don't simply pray for something you wish to happen. Pray for others, and pray even for nothing except for penance and His mercy. - *Oct 19, 2011*

We are called to live by His Word by loving others in deeds and action, for our words may be loud, but feeding and caring for all, louder. - *Oct 22, 2011*

Look not for reward nor recognition when doing good, but aspire to the journey of Christ and His Apostles (inspired by St Maximus). - *Oct 23, 2011*

Let us not bring God to the fore when we are spent. Rather, let us keep God in every step of our journeys, His strong arms behind us. - *Oct 24, 2011*

At the end, we face a mirror that reflects if we have loved God and loved others ahead of ourselves. Nothing else of the world matters then. - *Oct 25, 2011*

Draw no sword or malice against one who plots and attacks us, for God knows and sees the end in all things. In all pain, cry unto our Lord. - *Oct 27, 2011*

God does not wish that we inherit the pain and debt of hatred. God wishes that we receive the inheritance of prayers, kindness and love. - *Oct 27, 2011*

Thank you dear God, for calling a poor sinner like me to labor in Your fields. Grant me your Divine Mercy always, so that Your Will be done. - *Oct 27, 2011*

Dear God, thank You for Your frequent reminders, that we, your laborers in the field, are not to be afraid and carry Your love to all. - *Oct 30, 2011*

Dear brethren in the fields, as I pray for your loving labors, pray for me also, that we do our Lord's work gladly, proudly, tenderly. - *Oct 30, 2011*

Being satiated after hoarding much wealth is not contentment. Rather, it is being joyful and prayerful unto God despite being empty handed. - *Oct 30, 2011*

Profound evangelical journeys are found by following the saints who humbly walk the footsteps of Christ with deeds, prayer, and love. - *Oct 31, 2011*

All of us are ill, and the Church is our refuge and hospital. We are called to repent, pray, and care for one another towards healing. - *Nov 04, 2011*

When someone steals something from us, do not hate him, for God is love, and judgment is His. Pray for this person, and our own passions. - *Nov 09, 2011*

God erases our sins and scars and leaves behind only healing and beauty (adapted from St John Chrysostom, father among the saints). - *Nov 11, 2011*

The saints and fathers before us showed us the best way to evangelize the Word and to bring others to God, is through deeds steeped in love. - *Nov 11, 2011*

On the synaxis, may the Holy Archangels and bodyless powers of God, pray for us. May we grow closer towards God so we can behold joy. - *Nov 17, 2011*

Do not fall prey to thinking God is the lottery. Christ our Lord and God, called us to bear the labors of the Cross, so we may be free. - *Nov 21, 2011*

Beloved, despair not when harsh words are hurled our way, for our journey is the bearing of the burden of others. Keep praying. Keep silent. - *Nov 21, 2011*

Take joy in what seems to be mundane. For in the mundane, God is there and especially near, because we are not distracted by other things. - *Nov 25, 2011*

The Light of Christ is all around us, when we are in tearful prayer, when we move forward in reconciliation, when we partake in the Liturgy. - *Nov 26, 2011*

If we have the blessing to immerse in the fullness of faith, it becomes our vocation to love others more, not desert, scorn or hate them. - *Nov 26, 2011*

Let us of vocation, with prayerful love, say "come and see..." to all who are curious, lost, or desolate; for we preach the Love of Christ. - *Nov 27, 2011*

When we run out of words, beloved, do not be afraid, but make a determined Sign of the Cross, asking for God's mercy in the Name of Christ. - *Nov 27, 2011*

Trust in the infinite power of God. He makes the humblest mighty wonderworkers, simple ones mighty preachers, and the poorest mighty hearts. - *Nov 27, 2011*

The mercy of God is an infinite mystery. Beloved, do not be puzzled by mere appearances, and do not doubt the immense depth of His mercy. - *Nov 27, 2011*

The devil merely fans the raging fire burning from the coal in our hearts. Transfigure that heat till coal becomes diamond by humble prayer. - *Dec 05, 2011*

Do not imagine we are doing things "for" God. Rather, partake in the entire spectrum of Holy Mysteries and silent prayer, to be "with" God. - *Dec 09, 2011*

Let no act of man be our basis to judge or hate another. In the darkest of hours when rage drowns us, posture even lower, pray even harder. - *Dec 09, 2011*

Kissing an icon is prayer. It brings us spiritually closer to the communion of saints, who prays for us likewise, with love and faith. - *Dec 10, 2011*

Do not despise the mundane, for God may be found there. Conversely, do not be tempted by the flashy, for the devil often tempts with aplomb. - *Dec 10, 2011*

The lure of the ego is manifested by how often we judge or hate another. Conversely, the ascent of faith is manifested by how often we love. *- Dec 10, 2011*

When the storm is strong, be brave, because in the most potent of storms, we are stripped of all things except the pristine prayer unto God. *- Dec 14, 2011*

Understand that those who malign and hurt us carry more wounds and hurt than we do. Do not add to their wounds, nor ours, by similar deeds. *- Dec 15, 2011*

Pierce our hearts' passions and bleed them dry with the unresting prayers seeking and resting upon the Holy Name of our Lord Jesus Christ. *- Dec 15, 2011*

Beloved, in times of joy, let us remember and care for those in suffering. Do not forsake those we face, lest we miss Christ along the way. *- Dec 15, 2011*

Saints are rare as they found courage through their undying faith in God, to do things tremendously difficult and unfathomable by others. *- Dec 21, 2011*

Even facing the worst things, let us not trade our faith in God for anger or hatred. When we are frail, pray harder and leave all to God. *- Dec 21, 2011*

Beloved, if we try to see everyone as an image of Christ, we begin to find humility and an unceasing prayer of repentance unto God. *- Dec 30, 2011*

Beloved, we are not called to despair or to indulge in desolation, but to penance and prayer, for God strengthens us through challenges. *- Jan 03, 2012*

One who leans on God, will begin to find God's presence everywhere. One who rejects God, will miss God even if He is merely an inch away. *- Jan 05, 2012*

Christ is born, glorify Him! On His Nativity we rest our burdens and rejoice to the salvific love of God and the faith of our Panagia. *- Jan 07, 2012*

The passage of time allows us to remember the important days in history for us to encounter them again and again, like the icons in church. *- Jan 07, 2012*

Beloved, trust in the Lord, for His Will and Mercy prevails against any destruction and calamity, and His Church will sail through time. *- Jan 10, 2012*

Humility is only gained through adversity. This journey comes with our partaking of adversity conjoined with faithful and penitent prayer. *- Jan 15, 2012*

We only truly begin to live when we see God as the Sun Who nourishes us daily and lovingly, rather than we thinking the sun of ourselves. *- Jan 17, 2012*

We hope in the Lord in the face of adversity, because we know His Will is rooted in mercy and love, that carry and cradle us tenderly. *- Jan 17, 2012*

Behold the Mystery of the manifestation of our God, Father, Son and Holy Spirit. Behold the Mystery of our Christ made known to us, in Love. *- Jan 19, 2012*

When we pray, in calmness or in calamity, we are not alone, as our God looks upon us with mercy along with His holy hosts and the saints. *- Jan 19, 2012*

Love God and love one another is Christ's loving command; and it must begin with me. Lord have mercy as I stumble along in Your strength. *- Jan 26, 2012*

We make no apology for our faith in God, but to embrace the Will of Him who loves us. This life is His to mold and refine closer to Him. *- Jan 29, 2012*

Since muscles need exercises to grow, let us keep our tongues still. Instead, lean our ears and hearts towards God relentlessly. *- Jan 30, 2012*

Keep our faith as simple and honest as we can. Ignore the lures of detractors and cynics. Keep His Holy Name constantly close to our hearts. - *Jan 30, 2012*

Beloved, the tempest of the evil one is more clearly seen in these days. Be prayerful, be ever leaning upon the Strength of God daily. - *Jan 31, 2012*

"Instead of the tithes which the Law commanded, the Lord said to divide everything we have with the poor ..." - St Irenaeus (130-200AD). - *Jan 31, 2012*

"The rich are in possession of the goods of the poor, even if they acquired them honestly or inherited them legally." - St John Chrysostom. - *Jan 31, 2012*

In grave danger, pray more fervently to our Lord, because He indeed saves us from grave danger and roadblocks, and His Hosts fly to our aid. - *Feb 01, 2012*

While we grasp at however small our faith is, watch for the distractions in our lives that would derail us from our crawling towards God. - *Feb 06, 2012*

Beloved, love one another as Christ our God love us without prejudice, wholeheartedly, for unity is strength and leave judgment to God. - *Feb 09, 2012*

Sin is a sickness. Our calling as Christians is to heal the sick through the Church, not scorn or reject them (inspired by St Nikolai V.). *- Feb 12, 2012*

Failures are mere little pebbles along the long road that we are called to soldier on towards God, the eternal sun shining ahead of us. *- Feb 13, 2012*

We can only truly begin to have faith when we walk the journey of faith, struggle against our sins, and begin to care for and love others. *- Feb 15, 2012*

Beloved, submit joyfully to God's Divine Will of mercy, that His angels will tenderly and vigilantly guard our paths, however long or hard. *- Feb 17, 2012*

A tender love for another is not one of consuming fire, but a resolute and quiet strength given by the Mercy of God to stand behind another. *- Feb 17, 2012*

Carry the prayer silently in our hearts, for it resonates within and ascends, "Lord Jesus Christ, Son of God, have mercy on us, a sinner." *- Feb 17, 2012*

Peace is a priceless treasure and illumination Christ left to His disciples and us (John 14:27 & inspired by St Seraphim of Sarov). *- Feb 17, 2012*

"The bravest are the most tender, the most loving are the most courageous" – inspired by the bushido. *- Feb 20, 2012*

When we shield our wounds from God, He cannot heal us. Only when we expose our wounds to Him and cry to Him, His mercy and love can heal us. - *Feb 24, 2012*

Heaven or hell can be at the same spot where we are. It depends whether we meekly lean on God's will, or ravage the world with our ego. - *Feb 27, 2012*

Lord, grant us Your mercy so that we strive to always carry Your Truth to others with prayerful love, and not brandishing It as a sword. - *Mar 02, 2012*

We are not to seem more righteous than our brethren are in anything, but be zealous only in our souls, in secret (insp. St John Climacus). - *Mar 02, 2012*

Vainglory is the only sin not countered by an opposing virtue, and is the worst passion of all (insp. Mt 6:16 & St Ignatius Brianchaninov). - *Mar 02, 2012*

Let our hearts be silent in the face of dispute, for anger destroys charity, and pride destroys love for others. Instead, be deaf and pray. - *Mar 02, 2012*

When we are blessed with a scene of pure love, however unknown or incomprehensible, we are in fact finding God being there. For God is love. - *Mar 04, 2012*

Man looks at the exterior of a person, but God looks straight through to the person's heart. Is the heart prayerful and abundant with love? - *Mar 04, 2012*

The Church stands against all calamity and human will, because God's Love and Mercy prevails no matter what we do. He seeks us out of love. - *Mar 06, 2012*

We of the pastoral labors are called to be foremost, servants and ministers to all, joyfully in faith, for Christ showed us the Way (Mt 20). - *Mar 07, 2012*

Hell is just 1 letter away from Help. Hel"L" is a Loss of faith, while Hel"P" is like the Heaven of God opening up from our Penitent Prayer. - *Mar 07, 2012*

God never changes. He is eternal, and eternally loving. Let not falsehood or ego compel us to think God condemns us, which is our own doing. - *Mar 07, 2012*

The Lord admonished shepherds not to scatter and destroy, but to feed His people, to give them courage, and to comfort them (Jer 23:1-4). - *Mar 09, 2012*

Christ asked Peter, as He would ask all His laborers, that if they profess to love Him, they would joyfully feed His people (Jn 21:15-17). - *Mar 09, 2012*

Lord, gift us with Your tender Mercy and Strength, so that we can be dead to our passions, but joyously alive in loving You and others. - *Mar 09, 2012*

Unless we have immersed and lived another's life, we cannot know his heart. Only God knows the hearts of everyone from beginning to end. - *Mar 09, 2012*

Beloved, bear the cross of one another, for in that we lighten the load of our own cross, and the journey towards God becomes brighter. - *Mar 12, 2012*

It becomes easier for us to love one another, when we realize, God's love can only be universal and impartial to all His loved creations. - *Mar 12, 2012*

"Be kind, for everyone you meet is fighting a great battle." - St Philo of Alexandria. - *Mar 13, 2012*

We hope in our Lord, not for material gains, but for His Mercy so that we can still stumble towards Him despite our prideful failings. - *Mar 16, 2012*

Let us remember our Christian journey towards God is not one of luxury or relaxation, but one of extreme struggles against ourselves. - *Mar 17, 2012*

Lord, gift us with Your Mercy, that the raging and roaring tides in our hearts and minds can be silent so that we can hear you when we pray. - *Mar 17, 2012*

Just as God's Will is often a mystery to us, the works of His many saints may seem a mystery to us. Our own calling is to pray ceaselessly. - *Mar 18, 2012*

Let us remember the paternal admonition of St John Chrysostom, even in distress and pain, we pray, "Glory to God for all things!" - *Mar 20, 2012*

Lord have mercy! Gift us with the simplest and purest hearts, so our prayers are not fanciful, but simply our souls crying honestly to You! - *Mar 21, 2012*

God hears us when our hearts bleed with prayerful tears for another, for our faith is built on having tears and sweat for one another. - *Mar 22, 2012*

God's Grace is not partial to some, but abundantly ready for all. It is the sins of man that prevents him from receiving this Gift from God. - *Mar 23, 2012*

Even as the evil one relentlessly beats down the walls of monasteries, let us pray for the monastics, who pray for us as defenders of faith. - *Mar 26, 2012*

March on, beloved, for Christ is ever with us when we repent and pray, during this great march in the season of reconciliation and prayer. - *Mar 26, 2012*

Christ called His laborers to bear the pains of, and to lay down their lives for the Truth and the others, so all may walk towards God. - *Mar 26, 2012*

What could enslave us in the world then, beloved, when our sights are set high towards our God, and that all we hope and pray for is Him? - *Mar 28, 2012*

"He who is a stranger to peace, is a stranger to joy." - St Isaac of Ninevah. - *Mar 29, 2012*

"For he who does not love his brother whom he has seen, how can he love God whom he has not seen?" (1 John 4:20). - *Mar 30, 2012*

God is aware of our daily struggles and crawling towards Him. It means a lot to Him that we do struggle to Him, then simply give up trying. - *Mar 30, 2012*

He who strives to God with prayerful tears, God does not forsake, for His Love and Mercy is the sun which heals and nurtures back to health. - *Mar 30, 2012*

Our hearts need to be tender but resilient, even if it means getting hurt, for hardened hearts have no place for love for others or God. - *Mar 30, 2012*

It seems easy to simply give up one's faith because of strong dissenting voices. But ignore them and keep praying. God looks at our hearts. – *Mar 30, 2012*

St Maximos the Confessor, pray for us so we are vigilant and busy with our sins, and busy with our repentance and prayers for His mercy. – *Mar 31, 2012*

Beloved, the evil one and his lures are beneath the dust when compared to the Power and Love of God (inspired by St Hermas of the Seventy). – *Mar 31, 2012*

He of good and dispassionate judgment loves all equally – the virtuous for their rectitude, and the sinners out of compassion – St Maximos. – *Mar 31, 2012*

He who follows Christ in solitary mourning is greater than one who praises Christ in the congregation of men – St Isaac the Syrian. – *Mar 31, 2012*

Christ's commandment to love is to free us from hatred, so we may be gifted with loving all equally in imitation of God. – St Maximos. – *Mar 31, 2012*

If you pray for foes, peace comes to you. But when you love your foes, the grace of God lives in you, sufficient for salvation – St Silouan. – *Apr 01, 2012*

How do one discern a true union with God against an imagined or theoretical experience? Simply, loving the enemies – Elder Siluan, Athonite. *- Apr 02, 2012*

The man who has found love eats and drinks Christ every day and hour and so is made immortal – St Isaac of Syria. *- Apr 02, 2012*

Leave all human injustices to God, for He is the Judge. But for us, be diligent in loving everyone with a pure heart – St John of Kronstadt. *- Apr 02, 2012*

When the word "enemy" holds no more meaning to us, that is when we are walking closer to God just as we begin to receive His illumination. *- Apr 02, 2012*

Ubuntu (uMunthu) – I am because of who we all are, one family, children of God. *- Apr 03, 2012*

When the road ahead seems to blister and bleed us, keep silent, look inward, and pray steadily and penitently. God is there with us. *- Apr 04, 2012*

The sun always shines through for us, for storms are always fleeting. Be patient, pray and hope in our Lord, for He is always faithful. *- Apr 04, 2012*

Honor Christ by sharing your property with the poor. For what God needs is not golden chalices but golden souls – St John Chrysostom. *– Apr 05, 2012*

Most Holy Theotokos, our beloved Mother of God, pray for us who love you, intercede for us before our beloved Lord and Christ. *– Apr 07, 2012*

God is not a wishing well or a lottery, nor a cruel punisher. He is abundant and complete Love, and manifests in only Truth and Mercy. *– Apr 07, 2012*

Blessed is He who comes in the name of the Lord. We blessed you from the house of the Lord. – LXX Psalm 117:26. *– Apr 08, 2012*

Holy Archangel Gabriel, patron of those of us in communications and are messengers, pray for us! Let us remember that God is our strength. *– Apr 08, 2012*

My Lord and Christ, let us remember Your words, that we love others as we profess to love You, and that we love the least among us as kin. *– Apr 08, 2012*

Who are the least among us? They are the angels and saints, gifts of God to us, to show we are capable of fulfilling Christ's commandments. *– Apr 08, 2012*

Life is a journey of trials, not of punishment, but of purification and deification, a struggle to God. Pray with tears, find God in all. - *Apr 08, 2012*

The brightest path to our God, beloved, is often not the most obvious, and often demanding fortitude, a gift that God gives us when we pray. - *Apr 09, 2012*

Beloved, guard our hearts from the stain of any hatred; for hatred poisons and renders our faith corrupt and distances us far from God. - *Apr 09, 2012*

A servant of our Lord abides by His Will, and tends earnestly and faithfully to the needs of His people, however few, wherever they are. - *Apr 10, 2012*

Many scenarios in life can test our patience. Instead of merely reacting, ask ourselves if our actions will bring us closer to God, or not. - *Apr 11, 2012*

Christ is Risen! Truly He is Risen! Tá Críost éirithe! Go deimhin, tá sé éirithe! 基督復活了! 祂確實復活了! al-Masiḥ qām! Ḥaqqan qām! - *Apr 15, 2012*

More information

Father Raphael Phan is a bi-vocational ("tent-making") priest, spiritual director, writer, and software developer. His interests include pre-Nicene Christianity, early Christian writings (such as the Desert Fathers), liturgies, hesychasm, and philosophies. Please visit: www.saintflannan.org.

www.ingramcontent.com/pod-product-compliance
Lightning Source LLC
Chambersburg PA
CBHW061444040426
42450CB00007B/1201